# THE PORTRAIT MACHINE PROJECT

# THE PORTRAIT MACHINE PROJECT

***

# CARLO VAN DE ROER

Essay by Val Williams

DAMIANI FACTORY

Carlo Van de Roer
The Portrait Machine Project



Book Design, Philip Attar Creative

DAMIANI

Damiani
via Zanardi, 376
40131 Bologna, Italy
t. +39 051 63 56 811
f. +39 051 63 47 188
info@damianieditore.com
www.damianieditore.com



Printed in February 2013 by Grafiche Damiani, Italy.

ISBN 978-88-6208-268-6

# BEYOND THE MACHINE:
## Carlo Van de Roer's Aura Portraits

Val Williams

When Carlo Van de Roer embarked on a series of portraits using an Aura camera, he knowingly subverted traditional notions of the photographic portrait as a 'mirror of the soul'.[1] Aura photography, with its long history of scientific invention, and its contested position in psychic and New Age communities, uses technology which employs sensors '*that connect the subject to the camera, which translates biofeedback into information about the them, including character and 'how other people see them'. The camera depicts this information in the polaroid as color, associating/competing with a likeness of them, and as a printed diagram and description*.'

Carlo Van de Roer's interest in this process lies in '*the idea that a camera could offer an insight into the subject's character, or my relationship with them...the relationship between the camera, photographer, subject and viewer was something I wanted to explore*'.[2] His photography takes as one of its foci the space between intention and result, in which the unexpected may happen. It expresses a very contemporary interest in one of photographic history's great oddities, situating *The Portrait Machine Project* '*at an intersection of spirit and portrait photography... part of my interest [in this] is that aspects of spirit photography seem like excessive examples of ideas familiar to me in more traditional photography... the capability for photography to reveal an otherwise unseen insight is often mined in spirit photography...*'[3]

For Van de Roer, photography made with the aura camera has as its genesis those early technological experiments which produced spirit photography, but is less tenuous, more dramatic, more firmly rooted in a known and acknowledged methodology. It provides the context for a relationship between photographer, technology, equipment and subject.

Spirit photography, which relied as much on the imagination and the collusive wish to believe, could be seen as a 19th century attempt to both employ and outwit the machine, making claims that photography could perceive well beyond the limits of the mechanical process.

Its proponents claimed that objects or phenomena, invisible to the human eye, are revealed to the camera and transmitted to the photographic negative; this beguiling belief has interested photographers, ghost hunters, spiritualists and psychics since early photography (in itself seen as a kind of magic) performed the seemingly impossible task of producing an actual likeness of a subject. That early photography was seen as magical and mysterious was not at all at odds with it mechanicalness; inventions which emerged in the 19th century were baffling to those who encountered them, upending traditional belief, presenting a vision of the hitherto impossible. If photography could achieve the remarkable feat of producing images of the real world which were unchallengeably 'real', then it was surely just a small step to propose that this new and powerful medium could also see behind and beyond reality. Ungainly and unlikely as this early spirit photography may seem to contemporary eyes, it nevertheless poses an important question about photographic portraiture—while early photographs were seen as miraculous for being capable of producing a likeness, photographers soon began to desire that it should do far more than this, that it should provide insights into the very soul and character of the sitter. As photography gained maturity, photographers needed portraiture to transcend the simple representation of features, dress and body, to convey not only complex facts about the sitter, but also to distinguish the artist photographer from his commercial counterparts.

In a time of rapid and astonishing change, spirit photography could perhaps offer the reassurance that in the age of the machine and the changes that progress brought in its wake, mysteries could still exist. This was too, the age of the spectacle and as the scientist and inventor of the kaleidoscope, Sir David Brewster remarked: *'For the purpose of amusement, the photographer might carry us even into the regions of the supernatural. His art, as I have elsewhere shewn, enables him to give a spiritual appearance to one or more of his figures, and to exhibit them as 'thin air' amid the solid realities of the stereoscopic picture'.* [4]

If spirit photography revealed a desire not only to use photography's developing technology to engage the imaginations of a new and avid audience, but also perhaps to resist the idea of photography as simply technology, then aura photography perhaps played the same part in a mid 20th century society in which a rational modernism was dominant. What came to be known as Kirilian photography was first exposed to an academic audience by Semyon Kirilian in the late 1950s and brought to the attention of the West in the work of two US writers on the paranormal, Sheila Ostrander and Lynn Schroeder. [5] Published at a time when the counterculture was embracing many varieties of psychic and spiritualist practice, and when the public at large was highly aware of and fascinated by the perceived threat of the Iron Curtain states, the book held double appeal, and remains a classic. While scientists were interested in the phenomenon of the process that Kirilian had developed, spiritualists and psychics were attracted to the Kirilian process's seeming ability to transmit aura—the essence of the soul.

Aura photography has developed considerably since the time of Kirilian, and has now been assimilated into uses of the contemporary medium. The Coggins Aura Camera, launched in 1992, made aura imaging accessible, and attractive, especially to the psychic community. We are all curious about the unknown, about what can be revealed. Photography, with its ring of truth is commonly seen as a witness, a bringer of evidence, so the technology proved to be a fascinating one.

Carlo Van de Roer has taken this updated technology and has used it to present the dichotomies between what we already know, and what we would like to discover. He is aware of our curiosity about ourselves, and our desire to find clues to navigate our way through the chaotic narratives of modern life. His work assumes that we both have a notion of magic, while at the same time possess all the intellectual and social tools with which we can disprove its existence. Photography, which has been so stubborn in needing to find 'the truth', to bear witness, finds itself strangely outwitted by this peculiar technological quirk. After a random experiment performed by Joe Nickell at a Psychic Fair, Nickell expressed scepticism about the aura cam process concluding that: *'This tortuous process—involving obtaining dubious electrically stimulated data from the hands, extrapolating it by analogy to acupuncture to the entire body, translating the electrical frequencies into alleged color equivalents, and then substituting for them simple flashes of colored lights—can scarcely be called photographing the aura. As is typically the case with photographs of alleged paranormal phenomena, what you see is not what you get.'* [6]

That aura photography is contested in both its practice and in its meaning makes it fertile ground for the fine art photographer, in a genre where there are few rules and no entrenched expectations. Van de Roer takes part in a distinguished tradition of taking a genre which is allied to a particular school of thinking and transforming it into images which ask questions rather than seeking to answer them.

Carlo Van de Roer is less interested in the revelations which might be discerned in the results of aura photography, than he is in the relationships between maker, machine and subject, which have interested photographic historians since the beginnings of the medium. Van de Roer's photographs confound our ideas of the 'likeness', as his subjects emerge ghostlike through the hazy colour of the process. For Van de Roer, the very mechanicalness of the process, its assured results (however variable those results may be), is a vital part of the process. Drawing on the methodology of scientific imaging, he positions his practice as primarily non-interventionist: *'The aura camera is marketed as an accurate and precise machine, it's based on a land camera using instant film and has only one button, implying little mediation from the photographer. Here it also draws on the history of diagnostic imaging—technologies manufactured to reveal information about a person...'* [7]

But Carlo Van de Roer employs this optic science, this camera technology, with considerable freedom. He is not bound to the protocol of the experiment or the measuring of results; like all art photographers, he is free to make experiments where the results do not have to tally—there is no theory to be proved—only the artwork, what it communicates to its audience, how it makes its presence felt, how it changes the ways in which we are, are important.

The portraits made by Carlo Van de Roer and the aura camera are accompanied by the diagrammatic charting of aura analysis, and one is transported from the purely photographic to the idiosyncratic language of the New Age.

In *Miranda, July 2009*, the aura is violet: *'People see you as magical. You put out the highest vibrational frequency. What you want comes to you as if by magic. Enchantment, charm, sensitivity and deep spiritual understanding are the qualities most important to you.'* [8] In another portrait, *Martynka Wawrzyniak (two) 2008*, a haze of varying intensities of red surround the figure of a young woman: *'Creative, artistic–would best describe you. Orange represents energy with mental direction. You are alive, artistic, perceptive, creative. Constructive self-expression is important to you'.* [9]

Reading the aural notes alongside the photographs is intriguing; the language of positivity and self-help pervades them and stands in stark contrast to the portraits themselves, which have the ghostly quality of early photography, set in opposition to the modernity and youth of the subjects. In some, *Amani Olu, 2010*, and *Yoko Okutsu, 2008*, the subject is almost entirely obscured by the wraps of colour, enveloped and overpowered by the process. And although Van de Roer has made a clear division between his work on aura and the spirit photography of the 19th century, a connection can be made between those early spirit images, in which the ghostly subjects are both present and absent, and these very modern constructs.

In *The Portrait Machine Project*, Carlo Van de Roer asks a number of interesting and significant questions, some perennial to photography, others not. He enters the argument about photography's ability, or even mission, to portray the real. Although Van de Roer's subjects are unquestionably 'real' and often well known to him, his photographs serve to make them unreal, wreathed as they are in the coloured mists created by the auracam. These are straightforward portrait sessions, the subjects stand quietly, there are no props, no poses: it is the machinations of the camera which create the strangeness which envelops them. So Van de Roer's first question is about the presence of technology within photography, the usually ghostlike presence at the art photographer's party. Does the photographer take the photograph; does the subject create the aura, so poetically described through the positive speech of the New Age? Or does the camera and the technology that it contains, dictate the image? With an ever-expanding use of high tech production in large-scale photographic works and video by art photographers, the question of whether presentation overwhelms ideas is increasingly current.

Another pertinent question that could be asked of Van de Roer's work could be about the ways in which the work of art photographers both parody and celebrate the strange or outdated incursions of technologies into fine art photographic practice. Photographers still make pinhole photographs, and cyanotypes, still experiment with technologies which photography itself has far outrun. Van de Roer's photography is knowing, and treads that fine line between acknowledging parapsychology and drawing attention to its inherent flimsiness. Van de Roer, unlike those who market aura photographs as a quasi-scientific phenomenon, questions not only what this kind of portraiture means, but what we want it to signify.

But Van de Roer's photographs are not merely questioning—they are artifacts, objects of beauty and mystery, and try as we might to resist the notion of 'aura', it is difficult not to be beguiled by them. Would I be orange or violet or blue?

The colours dignify the subjects, make them otherworldly, sometimes almost invisible and mirror the mysteries of the first photographs which emerged via the miracle of chemistry and optics. *The Portrait Machine Project* transports us back to photography's early experiments, when everything could be believed.

Photography has stood on the sidelines of science and common sense since its early years. It has always been characterized by its excess. From Julia Margaret Cameron's riotous portraits of friend, relations and house servants, dressed up as angels, divas and saints, to Cecil Beaton's wild portrayals of British Society women in the 1920s and 30s, to the more recent work of artists including Gregory Crewdson, Anna Gaskell and Cindy Sherman photographers have felt free to toy with the real as soon as it is firmly within their grasp. Photography's task, from its beginnings, has been to take the real world and fashion it into a phantasmagoria of fact and fiction, infused with illusion. Carlo Van de Roer does this too, and asks us to take a step back and enjoy the magic.

Val Williams
London 2013

*Val Williams is Professor of the History and Culture of Photography at the University of the Arts London and Director of the Photography and the Archive Research Centre at the London College of Communication.*

---

1. This phrase was originally used by Virginia Woolf in 'Between the Acts' (1941) when describing the novel, and is frequently used when discussing photographic portraiture.
2. Letter to the Author, 2012.
3. Letter to the Author, 2013.
4. The Stereoscope, Its History, Theory and Construction. John Murray, 1856, London.
5. In Psychic Discoveries - The Iron Curtain Lifted: Prentice Hall, 1970 New York.
6. CSI: the Center for Skepitcal Enquiry Vol 24.3 May June 2000.
7. Letter to the Author, as above.
8. Extracted from notes from the photographer to the author, 2012.
9. Ibid.

# THE PORTRAIT MACHINE PROJECT

Carlo Van de Roer

CENTER
BLUE
Peaceful, Contemplative

```
             *B*
         *B*       *B*
       *B*   .***.   *B*
      *B*   * @ @ *   *B*
      *B*   *  ,  *   *B*
      *B*   *( v )*   *B*
      *B*    *   *    *B*
     *G*   .**   **.   *G*
    *G*   *         *   *G*
   *G*   * .*     *. *   *G*
   *G*   * . *   * . *   *G*
   *G*   * . *   * . *   *G*
   *G*   * .  * *  . *   *G*
   *G*   * . *   * . *   *G*
   *G*   * .*     *. *   *G*
   *G*   * .*     *. *   *G*
         *. *     * .*
         *..       ..*
```

RIGHT / LEFT

GREEN / GREEN

Healing, Teaching / Healing, Teaching

**CENTER** (EXPERIENCE) Color above subjects head.
Indicates what the subject is experiencing. It is the color that would best describe them.
--Depth of feeling-- would best describe you. Blue is the blissful fulfillment of the highest ideals of unity, of at-one-ness, of a reunion with earth-mother. It is truth and trust, love and dedication. Peace, tranquility, contentment, tenderness, love, and affection are the qualities most important to you.

**RIGHT SIDE** (EXPRESSION) Color on subjects right.
Indicates the personality that the subject projects outward and how other people see them.
Healing energy being expressed. An expression of firmness, of constancy, and resistance to change.
--Elastic tension--. Possession is regarded as increasing both security and self esteem.
The person putting out this vibration is willing to work, to gain wealth in terms of educational, cultural, or physical attainments.

**LEFT SIDE** (FUTURE) Color on subjects left.
Indicates what the subject is creating for themself in the near future.
Green is a growth color, it brings spring to mind. Like the new grass popping up out of the dark soil, small leaves stretching out from the barren branch-ends, as the last days of winter slumber fade and the renewal of life begins. Your future will be a growing time, a time for renewal, life springs forth. You are bringing in the healing energy to your life.

Yoko Okutsu, 2008.

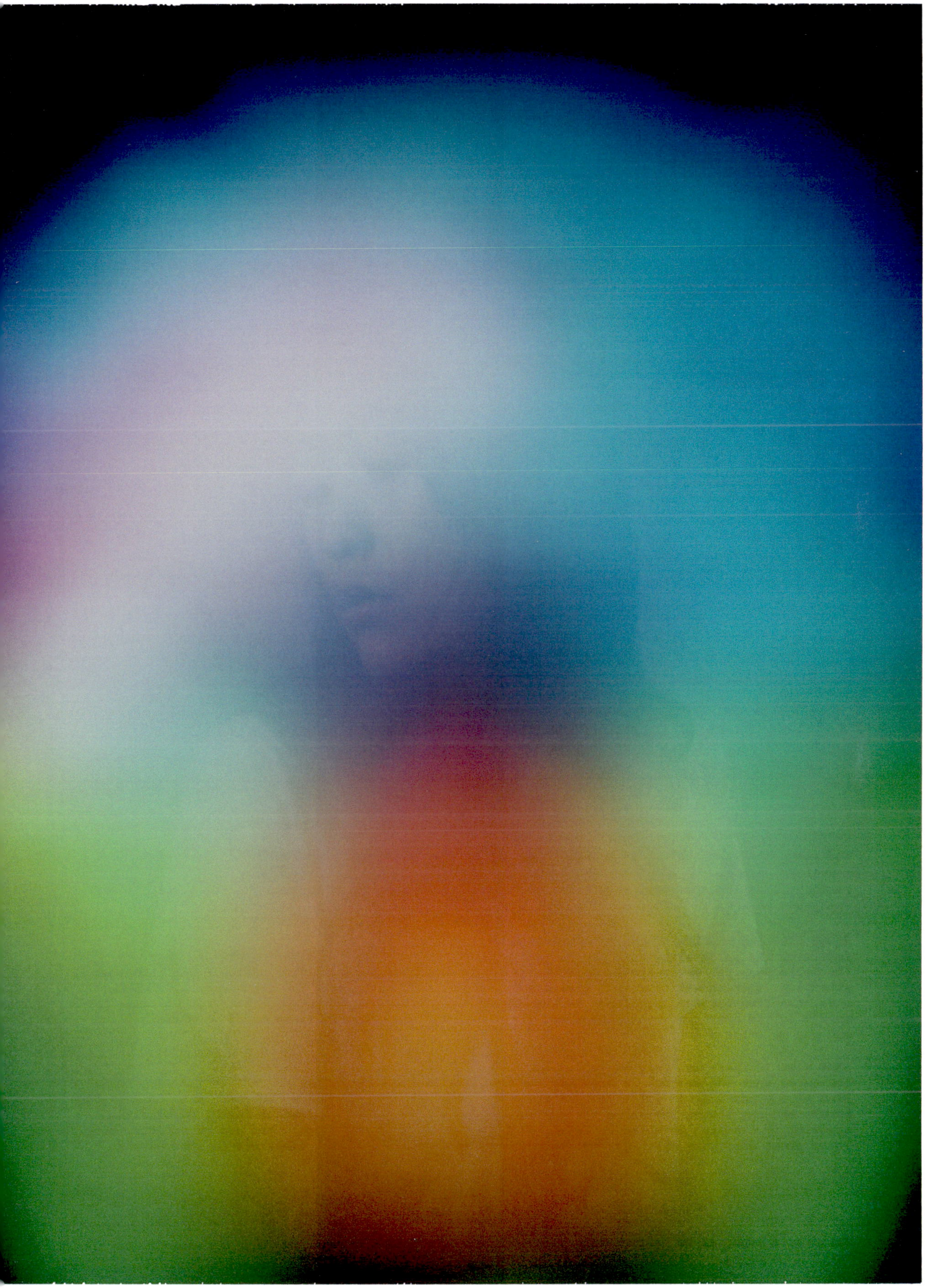

```
        CENTER
         GREEN
Healing, Teaching

          *G*
      *G*     *G*
    *G*  .***.  *G*
   *G*  * @ @ *  *G*
   *G*  *  ,  *  *G*
   *G*  *( v )*  *G*
   *G*   *   *   *G*
  *Y*  .**   **.  *B*
 *Y*  *         *  *B*
*Y*  * .*     *. *  *B*
*Y*  * . *   * . *  *B*
*Y*  * . *   * . *  *B*
*Y*  * .  * *  . *  *B*
*Y*  * . *   * . *  *B*
*Y*  * .*     *. *  *B*
*Y*  * .*     *. *  *B*
     *. *     * .*
     *..       ..*

 RIGHT              LEFT

YELLOW               BLUE
```

Sunny, Exhilaration Peaceful, Contemplative

**CENTER** (EXPERIENCE) Color above subjects head.
Indicates what the subject is experiencing. It is the color that would best describe them.
--Healing, elasticity of will-- would best describe you. Green is perseverance and tenacity. Persistence, self-assertion, obstinacy self-esteem, and teaching are the qualities most important to you.

**RIGHT SIDE** (EXPRESSION) Color on subjects right.
Indicates the personality that the subject projects outward and how other people see them.
The world sees you as cheerful. Gold is the brightest color. You may find yourself the center of attention, with others revolving around you. Radiant, and expansive. You represent relaxation, a release from burdens, problems, harassment or restriction. Your energy shines from you like the warmth of the sun, giving happiness and joy to all who stand in the radiance of your smile, and you do smile a lot.

**LEFT SIDE** (FUTURE) Color on subjects left.
Indicates what the subject is creating for themself in the near future.
Blue is a communication color, so you are a good listener, an intuitive listener, able to transform others through loving listening. It may be a good time to learn. You can be fairly certain when studying or learning on whatever level. If it is a ray or guiding light, you are being stimulated to learn about something which is important to your evolution. Peaceful times are in your future.

Christelle Imperial De Castro, 2008.

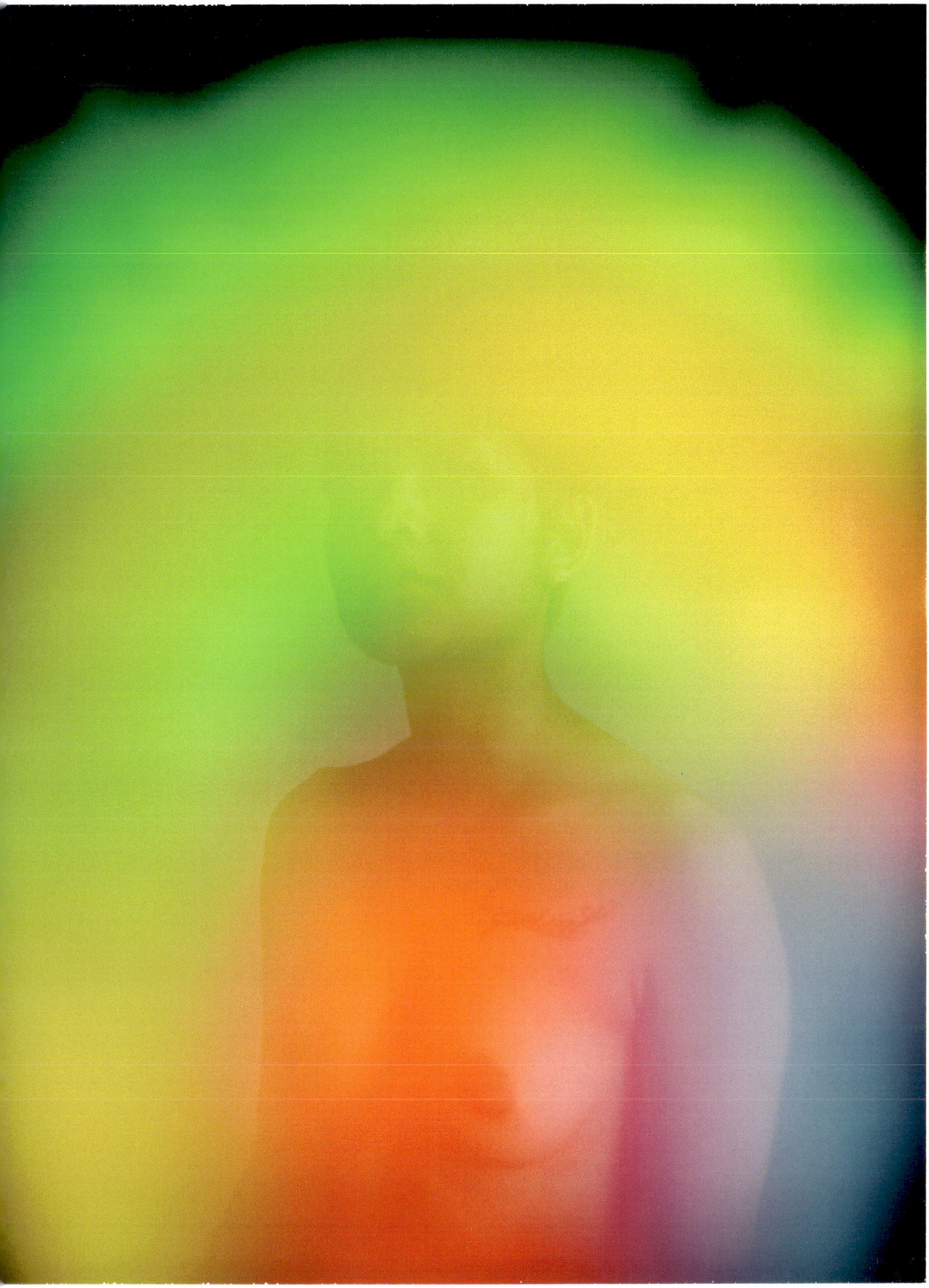

```
         CENTER
         VIOLET
   Mystical, Unifying

           *V*
       *V*     *V*
     *V*  .***.  *V*
    *V*  * @ @ *  *V*
    *V*  *  ,  *  *V*
    *V*  *( v )*  *V*
    *V*   *   *   *V*
   *V*  .**   **.  *V*
  *V*  *         *  *V*
 *V*  * .*     *. *  *V*
 *V*  * . *   * . *  *V*
 *V*  * . *   * . *  *V*
 *V*  * .  * *  . *  *V*
 *V*  * . *   * . *  *V*
 *V*  * .*     *. *  *V*
 *V*  * .*     *. *  *V*
      *. *     * .*
      *..       ..*
```

RIGHT — VIOLET — Mystical, Unifying

LEFT — VIOLET — Mystical, Unifying

**CENTER** (EXPERIENCE) Color above subjects head.
Indicates what the subject is experiencing. It is the color that would best describe them.
--Mystical unifying-- would best describe you. Violet is a high degree of sensitive intimacy, leading to complete fusion between subject and object, so that everything which is thought and desired must become reality. Enchantment, charm, sensitivity and deep spiritual understanding are the qualities most important to you.

**RIGHT SIDE** (EXPRESSION) Color on subjects right.
Indicates the personality that the subject projects outward and how other people see them.
People see you as magical. You put out the highest vibrational frequency. What you want comes to you as if by magic. You seem to get everything you need. A mystic union, a high degree of sensitive intimacy, leading to complete fusion between you and what you put your attention on.

**LEFT SIDE** (FUTURE) Color on subjects left.
Indicates what the subject is creating for themself in the near future.
Spiritual evolution is in store for you. Violet is a mix of blue --unlimited knowledge-- and red --activity--. Therefore spiritual activity will be in your aura. Violet brings unlimited knowledge. You will encounter the rays of guide energies, the highest vibrational frequencies will be distributed to you.

Miranda July, 2009.

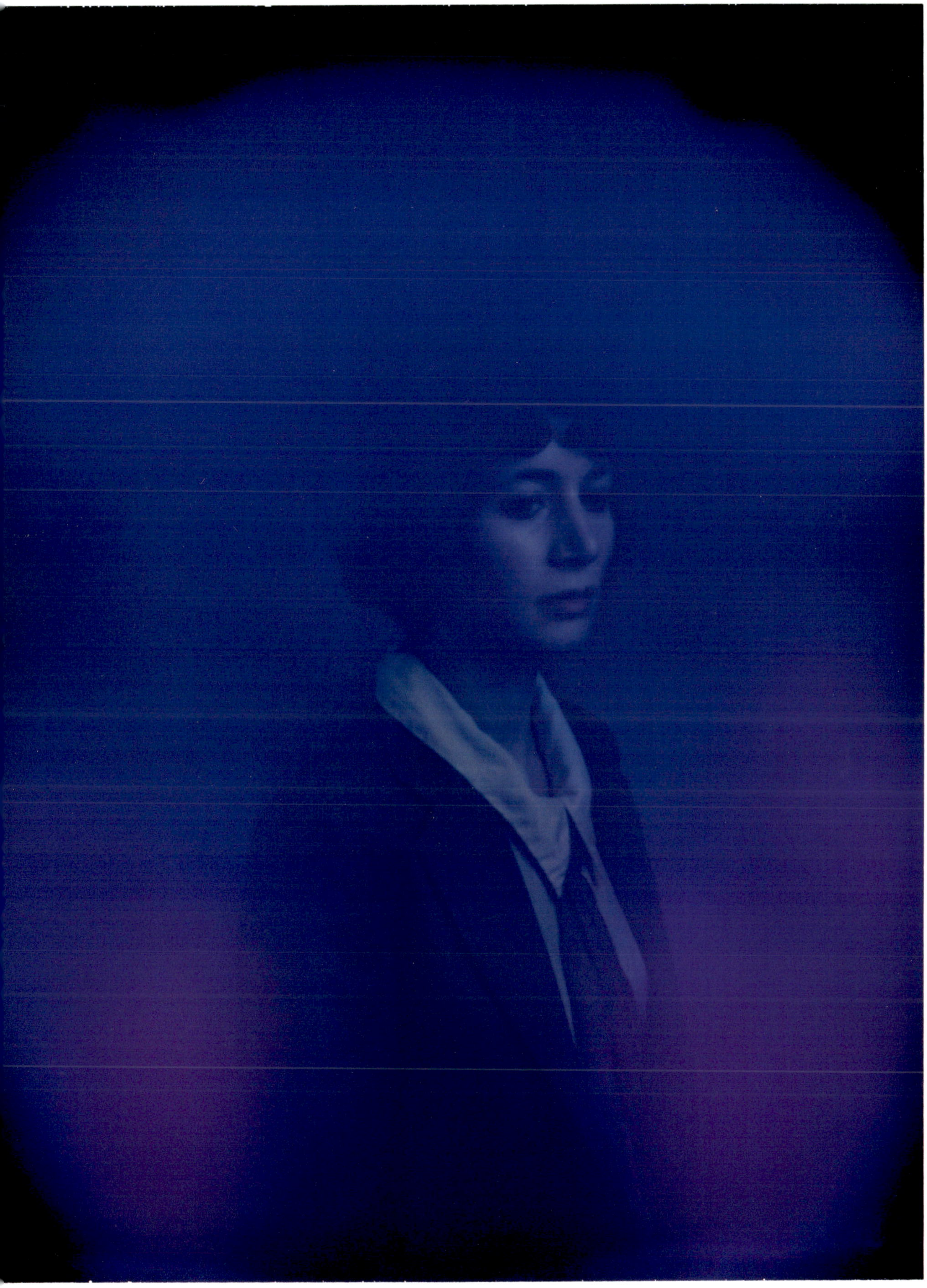

CENTER
ORANGE
Creative, Artistic

```
              *O*
         *O*       *O*
       *O*   .***.   *O*
      *O*   * @ @ *   *O*
      *O*   *   ,   *  *O*
      *O*   *( v )*   *O*
      *O*    *   *    *O*
     *O*   .**   **.   *O*
    *O*   *         *   *O*
   *O*   * .*     *. *   *O*
   *O*   * . *   * . *   *O*
   *O*   * . *   * . *   *O*
   *O*   * .  * *  . *   *O*
   *O*   * . *   * . *   *O*
   *O*   * .*     *. *   *O*
   *O*   * .*     *. *   *O*
         *. *     * .*
         *..       ..*
```

RIGHT

ORANGE

Creative, Artistic

LEFT

ORANGE

Creative, Artistic

**CENTER** (EXPERIENCE) Color above subjects head.
Indicates what the subject is experiencing. It is the color that would best describe them.
--Creative, artistic-- would best describe you. Orange represents energy with mental direction. You are alive, artistic, perceptive creative. Constructive self expression is important to you.

**RIGHT SIDE** (EXPRESSION) Color on subjects right.
Indicates the personality that the subject projects outward and how other people see them.
Creative endeavor, you are putting out and creating. Orange is a mixture of red --passion, force of will-- and yellow --cheerfulness--. The world should see you as up, happy, willing to work. You like to get out and have fun.

**LEFT SIDE** (FUTURE) Color on subjects left.
Indicates what the subject is creating for themself in the near future.
Activity generating energy is coming into your field. Orange is a mixture of active red and intellectual yellow, making a very creative future for you. Activity, wakefulness, and creativity unfolding. An opportunity to enjoy the sensual pleasures. Orange is known to give way to green, healing and growth, after the balancing period is over. Now is the time to go for it.

James Frey, 2010.

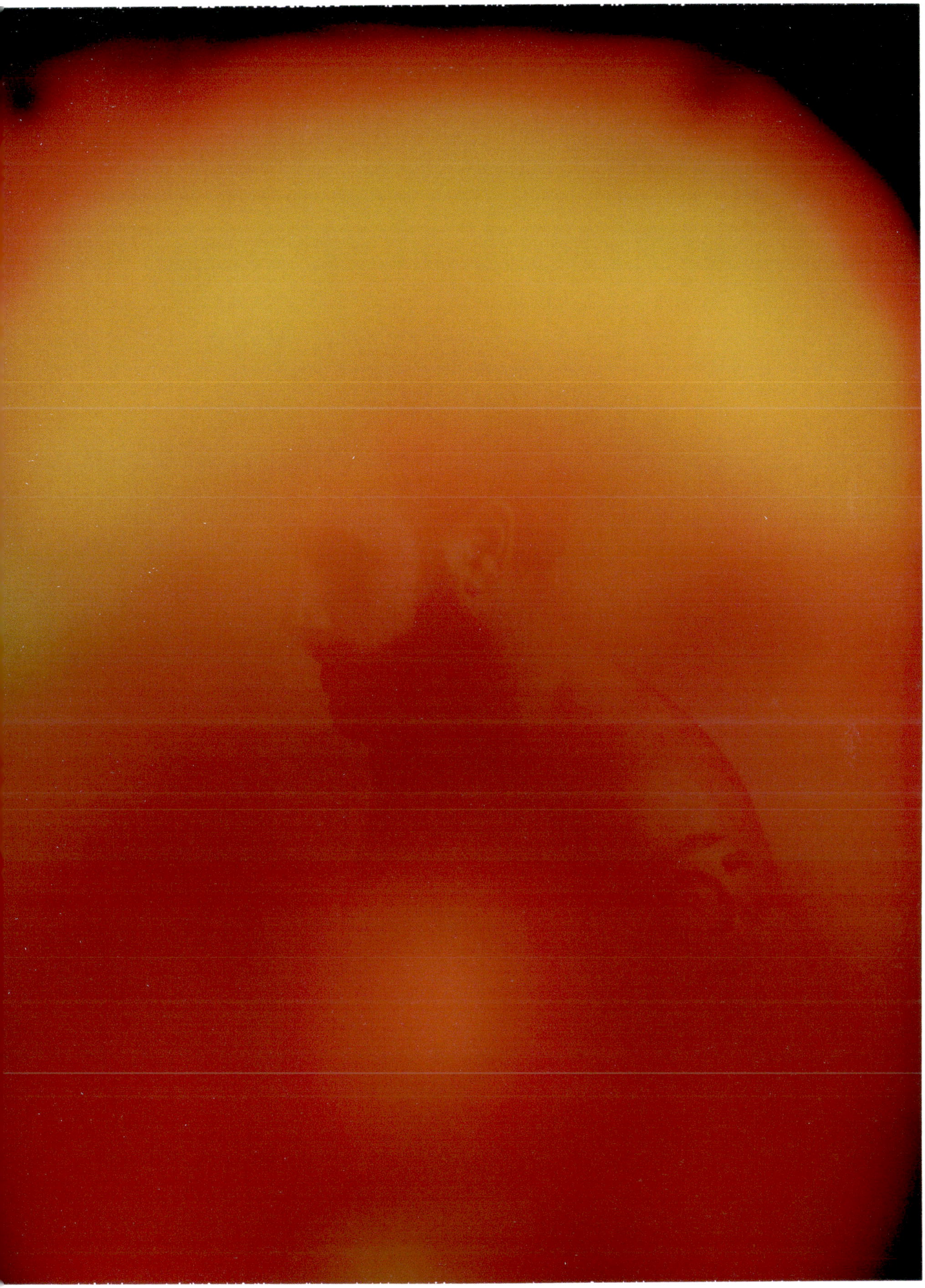

CENTER
BLUE
Peaceful, Contemplative

```
          *B*
      *B*     *B*
    *B*  .***.  *B*
   *B*  * @ @ *  *B*
   *B*  *  ,  *  *B*
   *B*  *( v )*  *B*
   *B*   *   *   *B*
  *G*  .**   **.  *B*
 *G*  *         *  *B*
*G*  * .*     *. *  *B*
*G*  * . *   * . *  *B*
*G*  * . *   * . *  *B*
*G*  * .  * *  . *  *B*
*G*  * . *   * . *  *B*
*G*  * .*     *. *  *B*
*G*  * .*     *. *  *B*
     *. *     * .*
     *..       ..*
```

RIGHT LEFT

GREEN BLUE

Healing, Teaching

Peaceful, Contemplative

**CENTER** (EXPERIENCE) Color above subjects head.
Indicates what the subject is experiencing. It is the color that would best describe them.
--Depth of feeling-- would best describe you. Blue is the blissful fulfillment of the highest ideals of unity, of at-one-ness, of a reunion with earth-mother. It is truth and trust, love and dedication. Peace, tranquility, contentment, tenderness, love, and affection are the qualities most important to you.

**RIGHT SIDE** (EXPRESSION) Color on subjects right.
Indicates the personality that the subject projects outward and how other people see them.
Healing energy being expressed. An expression of firmness, of constancy, and resistance to change.
--Elastic tension--. Possession is regarded as increasing both security and self esteem.
The person putting out this vibration is willing to work, to gain wealth in terms of educational, cultural, or physical attainments.

**LEFT SIDE** (FUTURE) Color on subjects left.
Indicates what the subject is creating for themself in the near future.
Blue is a communication color, so you are a good listener, an intuitive listener, able to transform others through loving listening. It may be a good time to learn. You can be fairly certain when studying or learning on whatever level. If it is a ray or guiding light, you are being stimulated to learn about something which is important to your evolution. Peaceful times are in your future.

Amani Olu, 2010.

CENTER
GREEN
Healing, Teaching

```
          *G*
      *G*     *G*
    *G*  .***.  *G*
   *G*  * @ @ *  *G*
   *G*  *  ,  *  *G*
   *G*  *( v )*  *G*
   *G*   *   *   *G*
  *G*  .**   **.  *G*
 *G*  *         *  *G*
*G*  * .*     *. *  *G*
*G*  * . *   * . *  *G*
*G*  * . *   * . *  *G*
*G*  * .  * *  . *  *G*
*G*  * . *   * . *  *G*
*G*  * .*     *. *  *G*
*G*  * .*     *. *  *G*
     *. *     * .*
     *..       ..*
```

RIGHT

GREEN

Healing, Teaching

LEFT

GREEN

Healing, Teaching

**CENTER** (EXPERIENCE) Color above subjects head.
Indicates what the subject is experiencing. It is the color that would best describe them.
--Healing, elasticity of will-- would best describe you. Green is perseverance and tenacity. Persistence, self-assertion, obstinacy self-esteem, and teaching are the qualities most important to you.

**RIGHT SIDE** (EXPRESSION) Color on subjects right.
Indicates the personality that the subject projects outward and how other people see them.
Healing energy being expressed. An expression of firmness, of constancy, and resistance to change. --Elastic tension--. Possession is regarded as increasing both security and self esteem.
The person putting out this vibration is willing to work, to gain wealth in terms of educational, cultural, or physical attainments.

**LEFT SIDE** (FUTURE) Color on subjects left.
Indicates what the subject is creating for themself in the near future.
Green is a growth color, it brings spring to mind. Like the new grass popping up out of the dark soil, small leaves stretching out from the barren branch-ends, as the last days of winter slumber fade and the renewal of life begins. Your future will be a growing time, a time for renewal, life springs forth. You are bringing in the healing energy to your life.

Terence Koh, 2008.

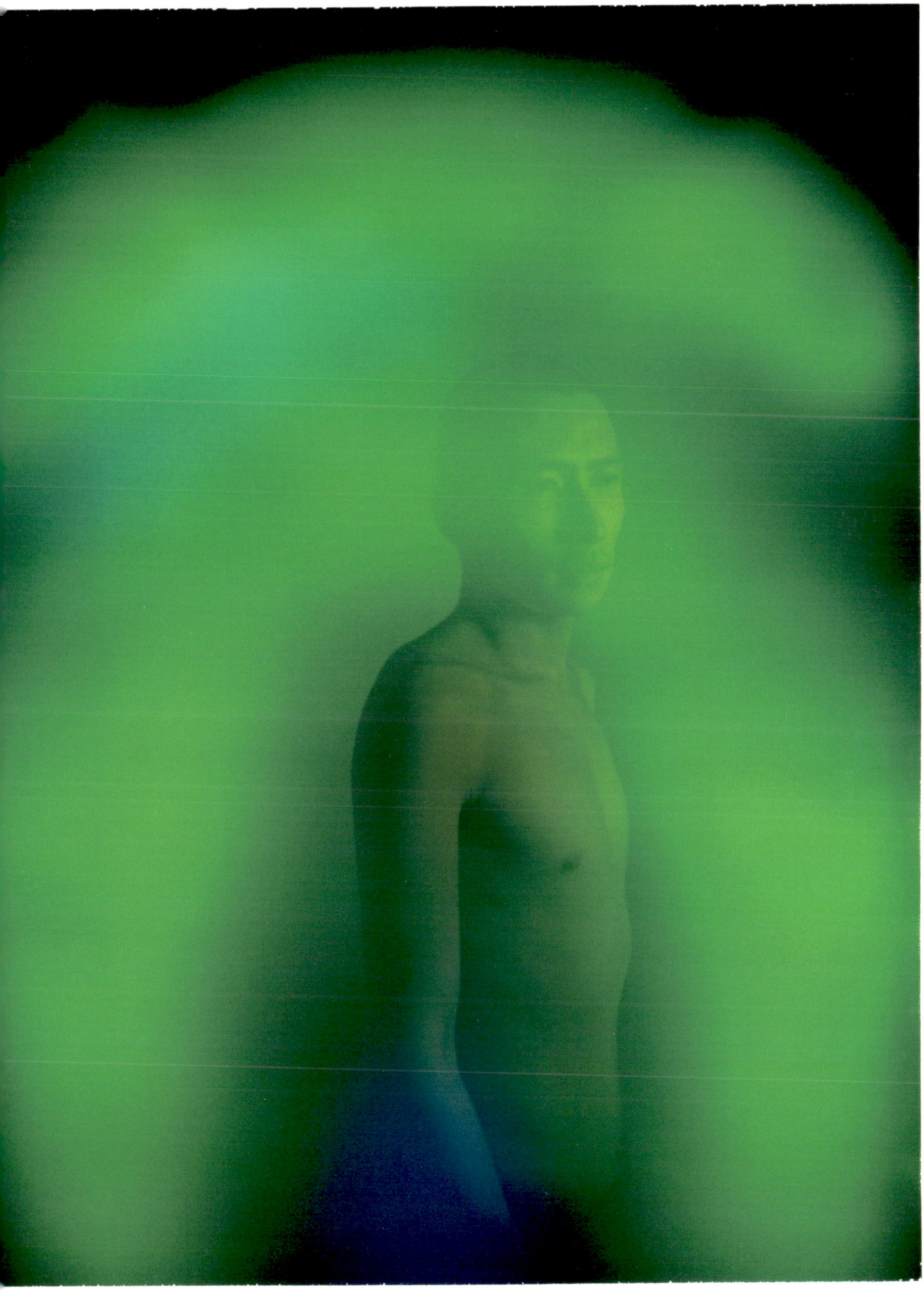

CENTER
YELLOW
Sunny, Exhilaration

```
           *Y*
       *Y*     *Y*
    *Y*   .***.  *Y*
   *Y*   * @ @ *  *Y*
   *Y*   *  ,  *  *Y*
   *Y*   *( v )*  *Y*
   *Y*    *   *   *Y*
  *Y*   .**   **.  *Y*
 *Y*   *         *  *Y*
*Y*   * .*     *. *  *Y*
*Y*   * . *   * . *  *Y*
*Y*   * . *   * . *  *Y*
*Y*   * .  * *  . *  *Y*
*Y*   * . *   * . *  *Y*
*Y*   * .*     *. *  *Y*
*Y*   * .*     *. *  *Y*
      *. *     * .*
      *..       ..*
```

RIGHT

YELLOW

Sunny, Exhilaration

LEFT

YELLOW

Sunny, Exhilaration

**CENTER** (EXPERIENCE) Color above subjects head.
**Indicates what the subject is experiencing. It is the color that would best describe them.**
Yellow corresponds symbolically to the welcome warmth of sunlight. Variability, expectancy, originality, smiling, and exhilaration are the qualities most important to you.

**RIGHT SIDE** (EXPRESSION) Color on subjects right.
**Indicates the personality that the subject projects outward and how other people see them.**
The world sees you as cheerful. Gold is the brightest color. You may find yourself the center of attention, with others revolving around you. Radiant, and expansive. You represent relaxation, a release from burdens, problems, harassment or restriction. Your energy shines from you like the warmth of the sun, giving happiness and joy to all who stand in the radiance of your smile, and you do smile a lot.

**LEFT SIDE** (FUTURE) Color on subjects left.
**Indicates what the subject is creating for themself in the near future.**
Your future is bound to be thought provoking. Like the rising sun, yellow brings warmth. Yellows are representative of the intellect. Each shade or tint of yellow expresses a type of function, ability, or expression of the intellect, from the craftiness of a mustard yellow, to the high thought of golden yellow. You approach the future with a sense of excitement and joy.

Caris Reid, 2009.

CENTER
BLUE
Peaceful, Contemplative

```
          *B*
      *B*     *B*
    *B*  .***.  *B*
   *B*  * @ @ *  *B*
   *B*  *  ,  *  *B*
   *B*  *( v )*  *B*
   *B*   *   *   *B*
  *B*  .**   **.  *B*
 *B*  *         *  *B*
*B*  * .*     *. *  *B*
*B*  * . *   * . *  *B*
*B*  * . *   * . *  *B*
*B*  * .  * *  . *  *B*
*B*  * . *   * . *  *B*
*B*  * .*     *. *  *B*
*B*  * .*     *. *  *B*
     *. *     * .*
     *..       ..*
```

RIGHT                LEFT

BLUE                 BLUE

Peaceful, Contemplative                Peaceful, Contemplative

**CENTER** (EXPERIENCE) Color above subjects head.
Indicates what the subject is experiencing. It is the color that would best describe them.
--Depth of feeling-- would best describe you. Blue is the blissful fulfillment of the highest ideals of unity, of at-one-ness, of a reunion with earth-mother. It is truth and trust, love and dedication. Peace, tranquility, contentment, tenderness, love, and affection are the qualities most important to you.

**RIGHT SIDE** (EXPRESSION) Color on subjects right.
Indicates the personality that the subject projects outward and how other people see them.
You put calm into the world, contemplation with a pacifying effect. Unification, a sense of belonging. --Blue is loyalty--. Blue corresponds to a depth of feeling. A relaxed sensitivity, empathy for esthetic experience. People see you as the calm of the untroubled sea.

**LEFT SIDE** (FUTURE) Color on subjects left.
Indicates what the subject is creating for themself in the near future.
Blue is a communication color, so you are a good listener, an intuitive listener, able to transform others through loving listening. It may be a good time to learn. You can be fairly certain when studying or learning on whatever level. If it is a ray or guiding light, you are being stimulated to learn about something which is important to your evolution. Peaceful times are in your future.

Taika Waititi, 2008.

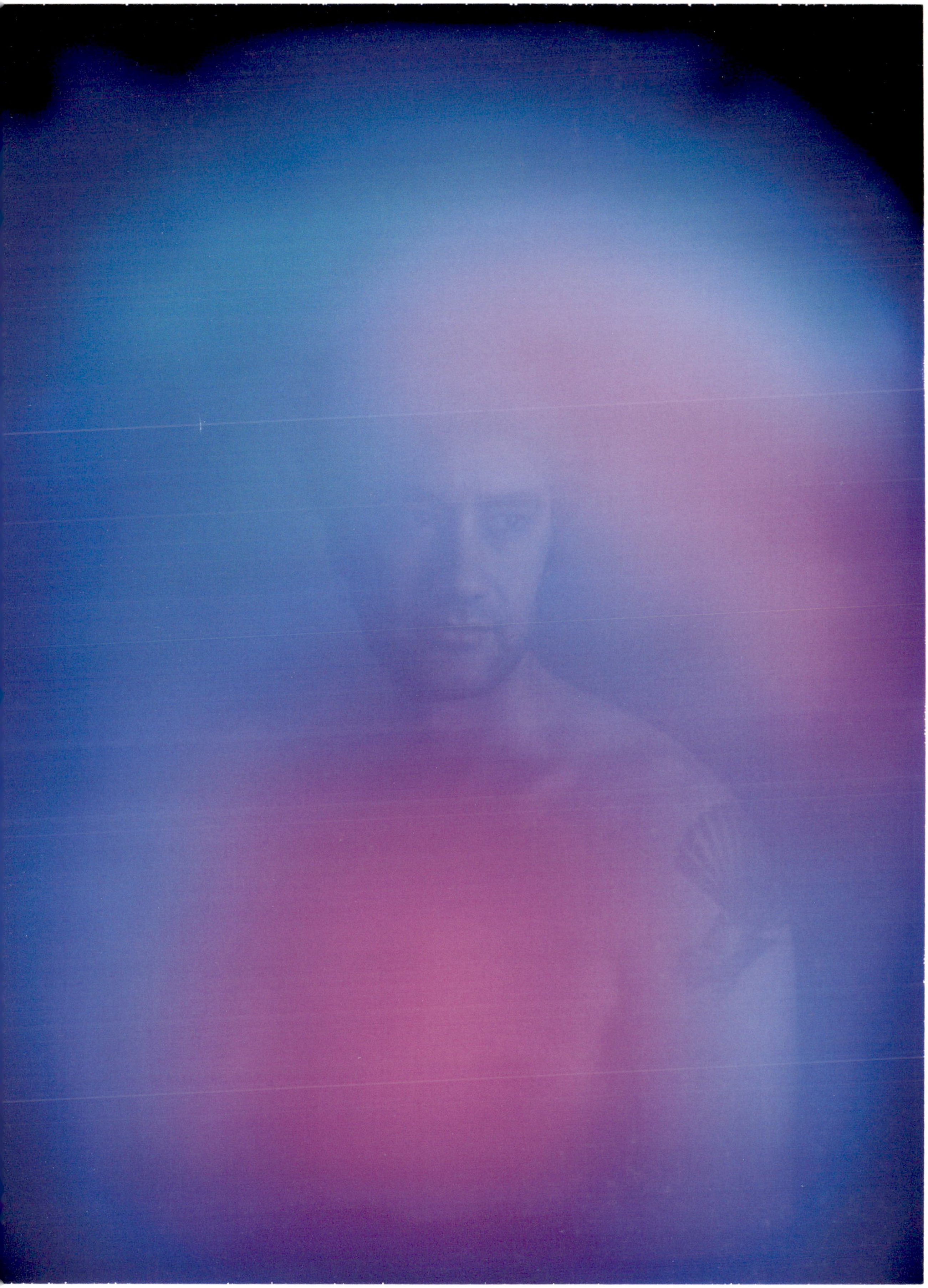

```
          CENTER
           BLUE
 Peaceful, Contemplative

          *B*
      *B*     *B*
    *B*  .***.  *B*
   *B*  * @ @ *  *B*
   *B*  *  ,  *  *B*
   *B*  *( v )*  *B*
   *B*   *   *   *B*
  *V*  .**   **.  *V*
 *V*  *         *  *V*
*V*  * .*     *. *  *V*
*V*  * . *   * . *  *V*
*V*  * . *   * . *  *V*
*V*  * .  * *  . *  *V*
*V*  * . *   * . *  *V*
*V*  * .*     *. *  *V*
*V*  * .*     *. *  *V*
     *. *     * .*
     *..       ..*

  RIGHT            LEFT

 VIOLET           VIOLET
```

Mystical, Unifying                Mystical, Unifying

**CENTER** (EXPERIENCE) Color above subjects head.
Indicates what the subject is experiencing. It is the color that would best describe them.
--Depth of feeling-- would best describe you. Blue is the blissful fulfillment of the highest ideals of unity, of at-one-ness, of a reunion with earth-mother. It is truth and trust, love and dedication. Peace, tranquility, contentment, tenderness, love, and affection are the qualities most important to you.

**RIGHT SIDE** (EXPRESSION) Color on subjects right.
Indicates the personality that the subject projects outward and how other people see them.
People see you as magical. You put out the highest vibrational frequency. What you want comes to you as if by magic. You seem to get everything you need. A mystic union, a high degree of sensitive intimacy, leading to complete fusion between you and what you put your attention on.

**LEFT SIDE** (FUTURE) Color on subjects left.
Indicates what the subject is creating for themself in the near future.
Spiritual evolution is in store for you. Violet is a mix of blue --unlimited knowledge-- and red --activity--. Therefore spiritual activity will be in your aura. Violet brings unlimited knowledge. You will encounter the rays of guide energies, the highest vibrational frequencies will be distributed to you.

**Alex Prager, 2010.**

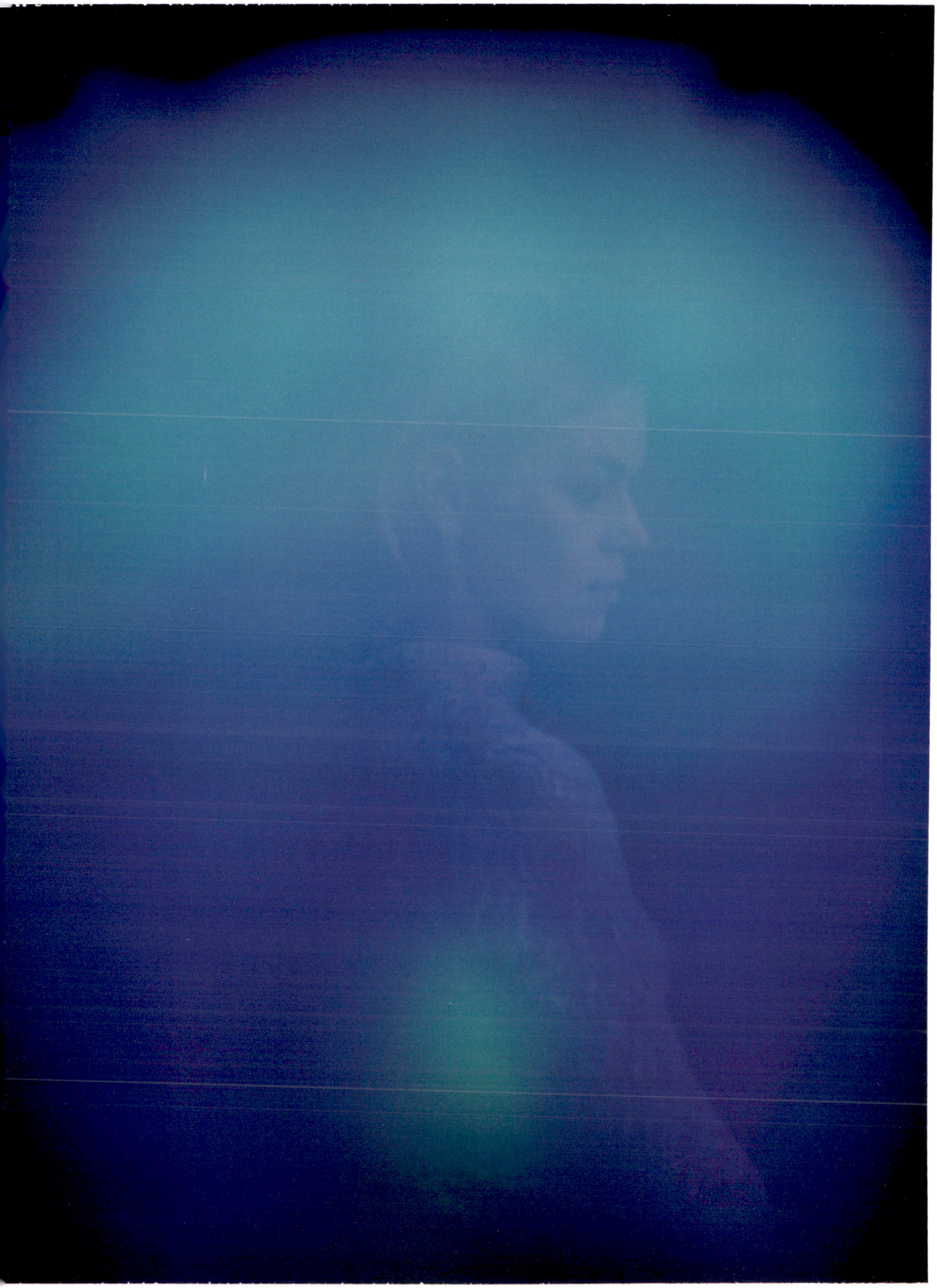

```
        CENTER
         WHITE
 Spiritually Motivated

           *W*
       *W*       *W*
     *W*  .***.   *W*
    *W*  * @ @ *   *W*
    *W*  *  ,  *   *W*
    *W*  *( v )*   *W*
    *W*    *   *   *W*
   *B*  .**   **.   *W*
  *B*  *          *   *W*
 *B*  * .*      *. *   *W*
 *B*  * . *    * . *   *W*
 *B*  * . *    * . *   *W*
 *B*  * .  * *  . *   *W*
 *B*  * . *    * . *   *W*
 *B*  * .*      *. *   *W*
 *B*  * .*      *. *   *W*
      *. *      * .*
      *..        ..*

  RIGHT            LEFT

  BLUE              WHITE
```

Peaceful, Contemplative                    Spiritually Motivated

**CENTER** (EXPERIENCE) Color above subjects head.
**Indicates what the subject is experiencing. It is the color that would best describe them.**
--Spiritually motivated-- would best describe you. White has the qualities of all of the colors.

**RIGHT SIDE** (EXPRESSION) Color on subjects right.
**Indicates the personality that the subject projects outward and how other people see them.**
You put calm into the world, contemplation with a pacifying effect. Unification, a sense of belonging. --Blue is loyalty--. Blue corresponds to a depth of feeling. A relaxed sensitivity, empathy for esthetic experience. People see you as the calm of the untroubled sea.

**LEFT SIDE** (FUTURE) Color on subjects left.
**Indicates what the subject is creating for themself in the near future.**
Very bright. A healing is coming for you and those around you. You are not a novice as the beauty of white light attracts all beings at every level of existence. These beings are very loving. They are there to help your evolution, a time to assist others in transition, or to make transitions yourself.

Kembra Pfahler, 2010.

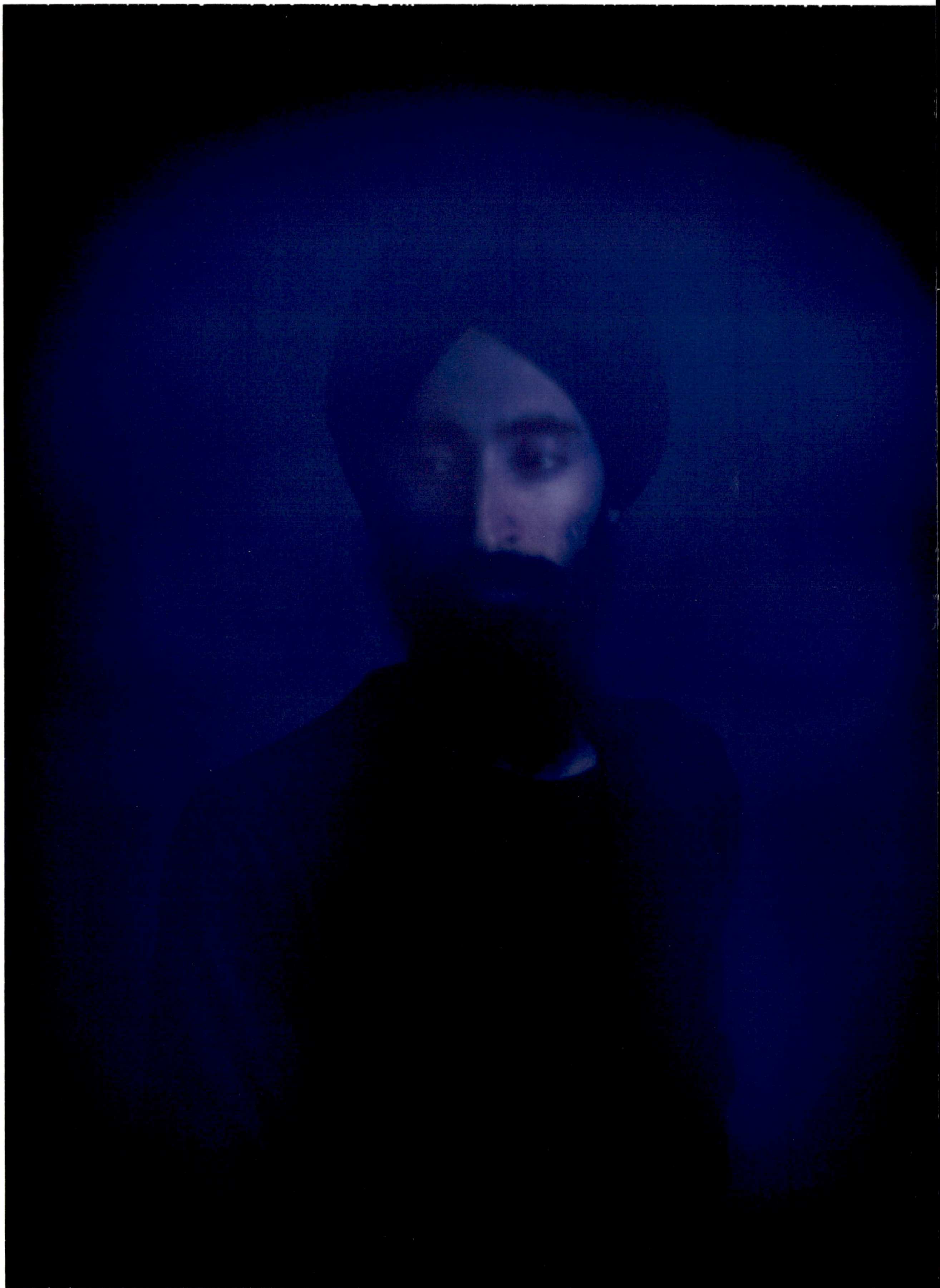

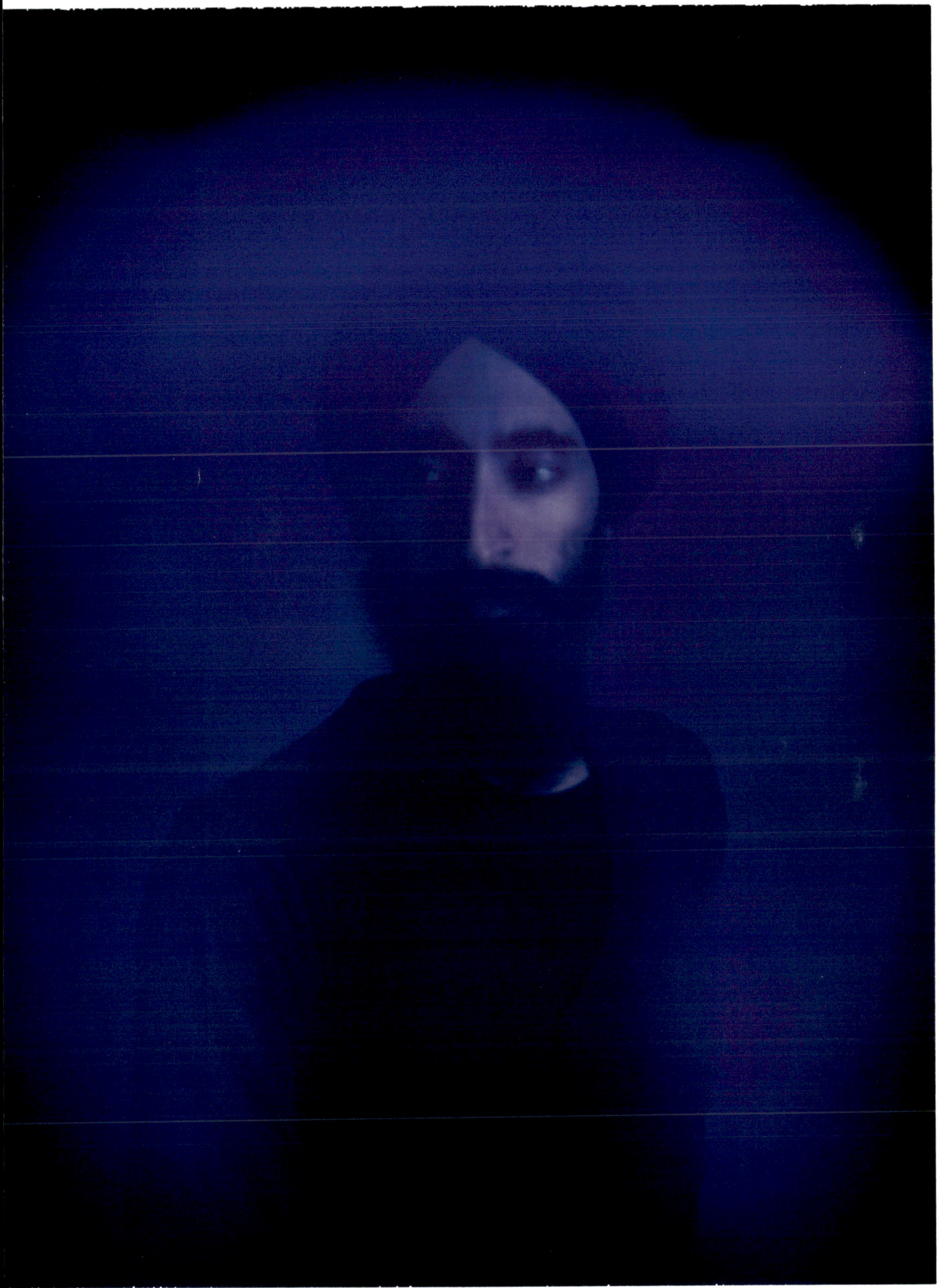

CENTER
VIOLET
Mystical, Unifying

```
          *V*
      *V*       *V*
    *V*  .***.   *V*
   *V*  * @ @ *   *V*
   *V*  *  ,  *   *V*
   *V*  *( v )*   *V*
   *V*   *   *    *V*
  *V*  .**   **.   *V*
 *V*  *         *   *V*
*V*  * .*     *. *   *V*
*V*  * . *   * . *   *V*
*V*  * . *   * . *   *V*
*V*  * .  * *  . *   *V*
*V*  * . *   * . *   *V*
*V*  * .*     *. *   *V*
*V*  * .*     *. *   *V*
     *. *     * .*
     *..       ..*
```

RIGHT — VIOLET — Mystical, Unifying

LEFT — VIOLET — Mystical, Unifying

**CENTER** (EXPERIENCE) Color above subjects head.
Indicates what the subject is experiencing. It is the color that would best describe them.
--Mystical unifying-- would best describe you. Violet is a high degree of sensitive intimacy, leading to complete fusion between subject and object, so that everything which is thought and desired must become reality. Enchantment, charm, sensitivity and deep spiritual understanding are the qualities most important to you.

**RIGHT SIDE** (EXPRESSION) Color on subjects right.
Indicates the personality that the subject projects outward and how other people see them.
People see you as magical. You put out the highest vibrational frequency. What you want comes to you as if by magic. You seem to get everything you need. A mystic union, a high degree of sensitive intimacy, leading to complete fusion between you and what you put your attention on.

**LEFT SIDE** (FUTURE) Color on subjects left.
Indicates what the subject is creating for themself in the near future.
Spiritual evolution is in store for you. Violet is a mix of blue --unlimited knowledge-- and red --activity--. Therefore spiritual activity will be in your aura. Violet brings unlimited knowledge. You will encounter the rays of guide energies, the highest vibrational frequencies will be distributed to you.

Waris Ahluwalia (One), 2011.

CENTER
VIOLET
Mystical, Unifying

```
              *V*
         *V*       *V*
       *V*   .***.   *V*
      *V*   * @ @ *   *V*
      *V*   *  ,  *   *V*
      *V*   *( v )*   *V*
      *V*    *   *    *V*
     *V*   .**   **.   *V*
    *V*   *         *   *V*
   *V*   * .*     *. *   *V*
   *V*   * . *   * . *   *V*
   *V*   * . *   * . *   *V*
   *V*   * .   * *   . *   *V*
   *V*   * . *   * . *   *V*
   *V*   * .*     *. *   *V*
   *V*   * .*     *. *   *V*
         *. *     * .*
         *..       ..*
```

RIGHT — VIOLET — Mystical, Unifying

LEFT — VIOLET — Mystical, Unifying

**CENTER** (EXPERIENCE) Color above subjects head.
Indicates what the subject is experiencing. It is the color that would best describe them.
--Mystical unifying-- would best describe you. Violet is a high degree of sensitive intimacy, leading to complete fusion between subject and object, so that everything which is thought and desired must become reality. Enchantment, charm, sensitivity and deep spiritual understanding are the qualities most important to you.

**RIGHT SIDE** (EXPRESSION) Color on subjects right.
Indicates the personality that the subject projects outward and how other people see them.
People see you as magical. You put out the highest vibrational frequency. What you want comes to you as if by magic. You seem to get everything you need. A mystic union, a high degree of sensitive intimacy, leading to complete fusion between you and what you put your attention on.

**LEFT SIDE** (FUTURE) Color on subjects left.
Indicates what the subject is creating for themself in the near future.
Spiritual evolution is in store for you. Violet is a mix of blue --unlimited knowledge-- and red --activity--. Therefore spiritual activity will be in your aura. Violet brings unlimited knowledge. You will encounter the rays of guide energies, the highest vibrational frequencies will be distributed to you.

Waris Ahluwalia (Two), 2011.

CENTER
GREEN
Healing, Teaching

```
            *G*
        *G*      *G*
      *G*   .***.   *G*
     *G*   * @ @ *   *G*
     *G*   *  ,  *   *G*
     *G*   *( v )*   *G*
     *G*    *   *    *G*
    *G*   .**   **.   *B*
   *G*   *         *   *B*
  *G*   * .*     *. *   *B*
  *G*   * . *   * . *   *B*
  *G*   * . *   * . *   *B*
  *G*   * .  * *  . *   *B*
  *G*   * . *   * . *   *B*
  *G*   * .*     *. *   *B*
  *G*   * .*     *. *   *B*
        *. *     * .*
        *..       ..*
```

RIGHT — GREEN — Healing, Teaching

LEFT — BLUE — Peaceful, Contemplative

**CENTER** (EXPERIENCE) Color above subjects head.
**Indicates what the subject is experiencing. It is the color that would best describe them.**
--Healing, elasticity of will-- would best describe you. Green is perseverance and tenacity. Persistence, self-assertion, obstinacy self-esteem, and teaching are the qualities most important to you.

**RIGHT SIDE** (EXPRESSION) Color on subjects right.
**Indicates the personality that the subject projects outward and how other people see them.**
Healing energy being expressed. An expression of firmness, of constancy, and resistance to change. --Elastic tension--. Possession is regarded as increasing both security and self esteem.
The person putting out this vibration is willing to work, to gain wealth in terms of educational, cultural, or physical attainments.

**LEFT SIDE** (FUTURE) Color on subjects left.
**Indicates what the subject is creating for themself in the near future.**
Blue is a communication color, so you are a good listener, an intuitive listener, able to transform others through loving listening. It may be a good time to learn. You can be fairly certain when studying or learning on whatever level. If it is a ray or guiding light, you are being stimulated to learn about something which is important to your evolution. Peaceful times are in your future.

Yana Toyber, 2011.

```
          CENTER
           BLUE
  Peaceful, Contemplative

          *B*
      *B*     *B*
    *B*  .***.  *B*
   *B*  * @ @ *  *B*
   *B*  *  ,  *  *B*
   *B*  *( v )*  *B*
   *B*   *   *   *B*
  *Y*  .**   **.  *B*
 *Y*  *         *  *B*
*Y*  * .*     *. *  *B*
*Y*  * . *   * . *  *B*
*Y*  * . *   * . *  *B*
*Y*  * .  * *  . *  *B*
*Y*  * . *   * . *  *B*
*Y*  * .*     *. *  *B*
*Y*  * .*     *. *  *B*
     *. *     * .*
     *..       ..*

 RIGHT            LEFT

YELLOW             BLUE
```

Sunny, Exhilaration                Peaceful, Contemplative

**CENTER** (EXPERIENCE) Color above subjects head.
**Indicates what the subject is experiencing. It is the color that would best describe them.**
--Depth of feeling-- would best describe you. Blue is the blissful fulfillment of the highest ideals of unity, of at-one-ness, of a reunion with earth-mother. It is truth and trust, love and dedication. Peace, tranquility, contentment, tenderness, love, and affection are the qualities most important to you.

**RIGHT SIDE.** (EXPRESSION) Color on subjects right.
**Indicates the personality that the subject projects outward and how other people see them.**
The world sees you as cheerful. Gold is the brightest color. You may find yourself the center of attention, with others revolving around you. Radiant, and expansive. You represent relaxation, a release from burdens, problems, harassment or restriction. Your energy shines from you like the warmth of the sun, giving happiness and joy to all who stand in the radiance of your smile, and you do smile a lot.

**LEFT SIDE** (FUTURE) Color on subjects left.
**Indicates what the subject is creating for themself in the near future.**
Blue is a communication color, so you are a good listener, an intuitive listener, able to transform others through loving listening. It may be a good time to learn. You can be fairly certain when studying or learning on whatever level. If it is a ray or guiding light, you are being stimulated to learn about something which is important to your evolution. Peaceful times are in your future.

Philippe Starck, 2010.

```
           CENTER
           GREEN
     Healing, Teaching

          *G*
      *G*     *G*
    *G*  .***.  *G*
   *G*  * @ @ *  *G*
   *G*  *  ,  *  *G*
   *G*  *( v )*  *G*
   *G*   *   *   *G*
  *G*  .**   **.  *W*
 *G*  *         *  *W*
*G*  * .*     *. *  *W*
*G*  * . *   * . *  *W*
*G*  * . *   * . *  *W*
*G*  * .  * *  . *  *W*
*G*  * . *   * . *  *W*
*G*  * .*     *. *  *W*
*G*  * .*     *. *  *W*
     *. *     * .*
     *..       ..*

 RIGHT             LEFT

 GREEN              WHITE
```

Healing, Teaching Spiritually Motivated

**CENTER** (EXPERIENCE) Color above subjects head.
**Indicates what the subject is experiencing. It is the color that would best describe them.**
--Healing, elasticity of will-- would best describe you. Green is perseverance and tenacity. Persistence, self-assertion, obstinacy self-esteem, and teaching are the qualities most important to you.

**RIGHT SIDE** (EXPRESSION) Color on subjects right.
**Indicates the personality that the subject projects outward and how other people see them.**
Healing energy being expressed. An expression of firmness, of constancy, and resistance to change. --Elastic tension--. Possession is regarded as increasing both security and self esteem. The person putting out this vibration is willing to work, to gain wealth in terms of educational, cultural, or physical attainments.

**LEFT SIDE** (FUTURE) Color on subjects left.
**Indicates what the subject is creating for themself in the near future.**
Very bright. A healing is coming for you and those around you. You are not a novice as the beauty of white light attracts all beings at every level of existence. These beings are very loving. They are there to help your evolution, a time to assist others in transition, or to make transitions yourself.

Aurel Schmidt, 2009.

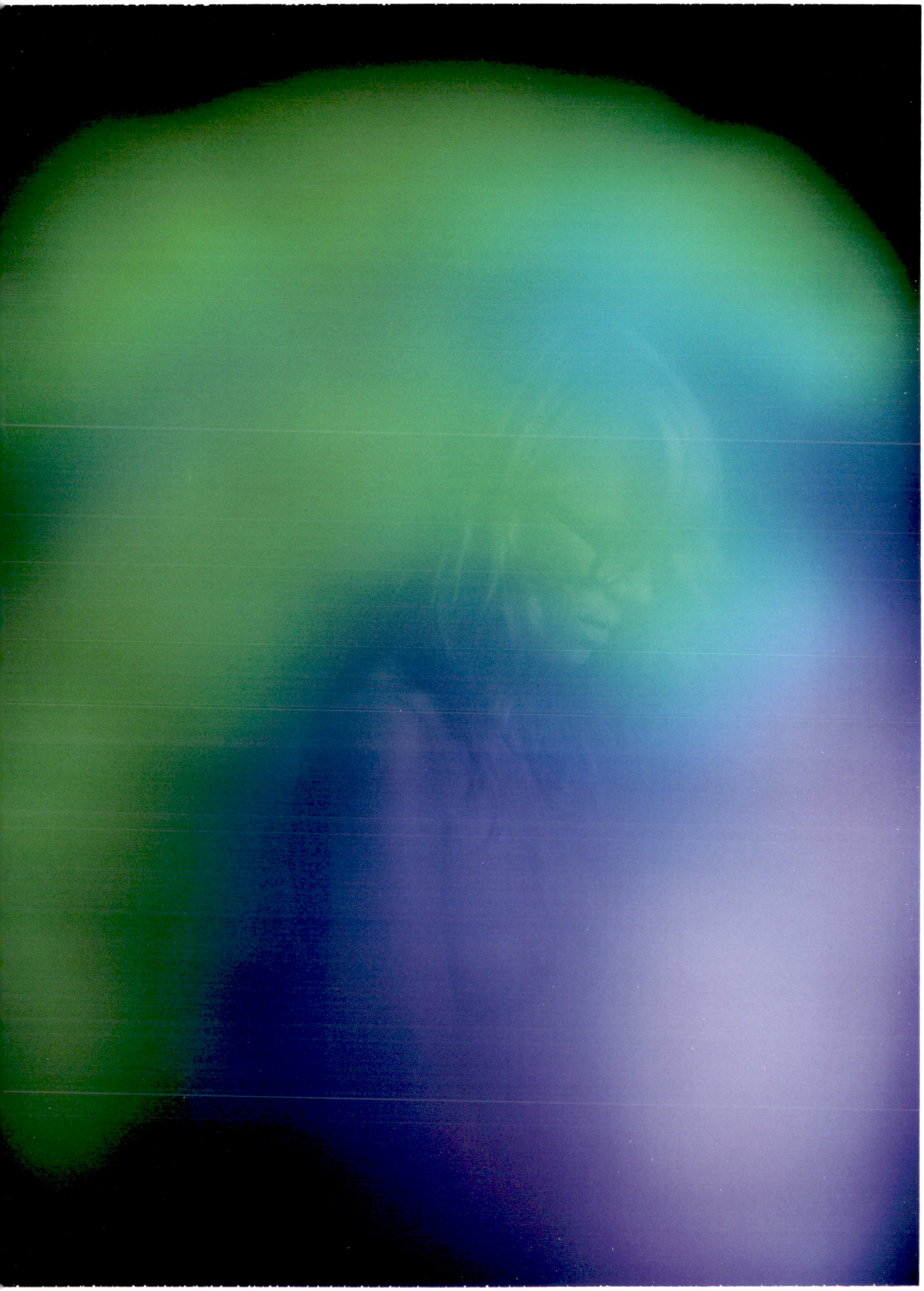

CENTER
GREEN
Healing, Teaching

```
          *G*
      *G*     *G*
    *G*  .***.  *G*
   *G*  * @ @ *  *G*
   *G*  *  ,  *  *G*
   *G*  *( v )*  *G*
   *G*   *   *   *G*
  *B*  .**   **.  *G*
 *B*  *         *  *G*
*B*  * .*     *. *  *G*
*B*  * . *   * . *  *G*
*B*  * . *   * . *  *G*
*B*  * .  * *  . *  *G*
*B*  * . *   * . *  *G*
*B*  * .*     *. *  *G*
*B*  * .*     *. *  *G*
     *. *     * .*
     *..       ..*
```

RIGHT LEFT

BLUE GREEN

Peaceful, Contemplative Healing, Teaching

CENTER (EXPERIENCE) Color above subjects head.
Indicates what the subject is experiencing. It is the color that would best describe them.
--Healing, elasticity of will-- would best describe you. Green is perseverance and tenacity. Persistence, self-assertion, obstinacy self-esteem, and teaching are the qualities most important to you.

RIGHT SIDE (EXPRESSION) Color on subjects right.
Indicates the personality that the subject projects outward and how other people see them.
You put calm into the world, contemplation with a pacifying effect. Unification, a sense of belonging. --Blue is loyalty--. Blue corresponds to a depth of feeling. A relaxed sensitivity, empathy for esthetic experience. People see you as the calm of the untroubled sea.

LEFT SIDE (FUTURE) Color on subjects left.
Indicates what the subject is creating for themself in the near future.
Green is a growth color, it brings spring to mind. Like the new grass popping up out of the dark soil, small leaves stretching out from the barren branch-ends, as the last days of winter slumber fade and the renewal of life begins. Your future will be a growing time, a time for renewal, life springs forth. You are bringing in the healing energy to your life.

Lorenzo Martone, 2009.

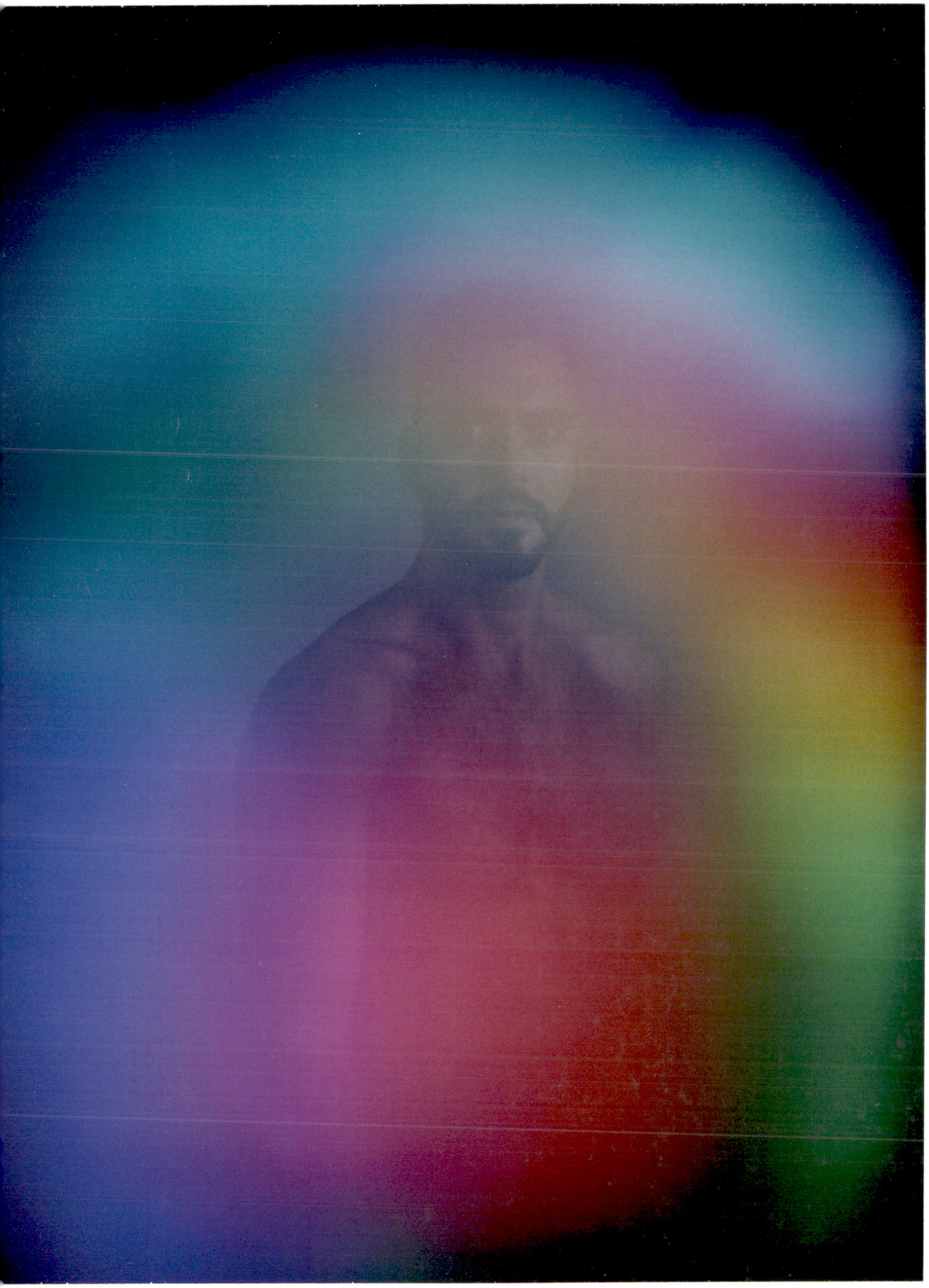

```
              CENTER
              YELLOW
        Sunny, Exhilaration

                *Y*
           *Y*       *Y*
         *Y*   .***.   *Y*
        *Y*   * @ @ *   *Y*
        *Y*   *  ,  *   *Y*
        *Y*   *( v )*   *Y*
        *Y*    *   *    *Y*
      *W*   .**     **.   *B*
     *W*   *             *   *B*
    *W*   * .*         *. *   *B*
    *W*   * . *       * . *   *B*
    *W*   * . *       * . *   *B*
    *W*   * .   * *     . *   *B*
    *W*   * . *       * . *   *B*
    *W*   * .*         *. *   *B*
    *W*   * .*         *. *   *B*
          *. *         * .*
          *..           ..*

       RIGHT                LEFT

       WHITE                BLUE

Spiritually Motivated              Peaceful, Contemplative
```

**CENTER** (EXPERIENCE) Color above subjects head.
**Indicates what the subject is experiencing. It is the color that would best describe them.**
Yellow corresponds symbolically to the welcome warmth of sunlight. Variability, expectancy, originality, smiling, and exhilaration are the qualities most important to you.

**RIGHT SIDE** (EXPRESSION) Color on Subjects right.
**Indicates the personality that the subject projects outward and how other people see them.**
You have a healing effect on all in your field. White is a mixture of all the colors. You emit all the qualities at the same time. Though white tends to be unstable, like a supernova, it is a healing experience. You could be a spiritual leader.

**LEFT SIDE** (FUTURE) Color on subjects left.
**Indicates what the subject is creating for themself in the near future.**
Blue is a communication color, so you are a good listener, an intuitive listener, able to transform others through loving listening. It may be a good time to learn. You can be fairly certain when studying or learning on whatever level. If it is a ray or guiding light, you are being stimulated to learn about something which is important to your evolution. Peaceful times are in your future.

Carlo McCormick, 2009.

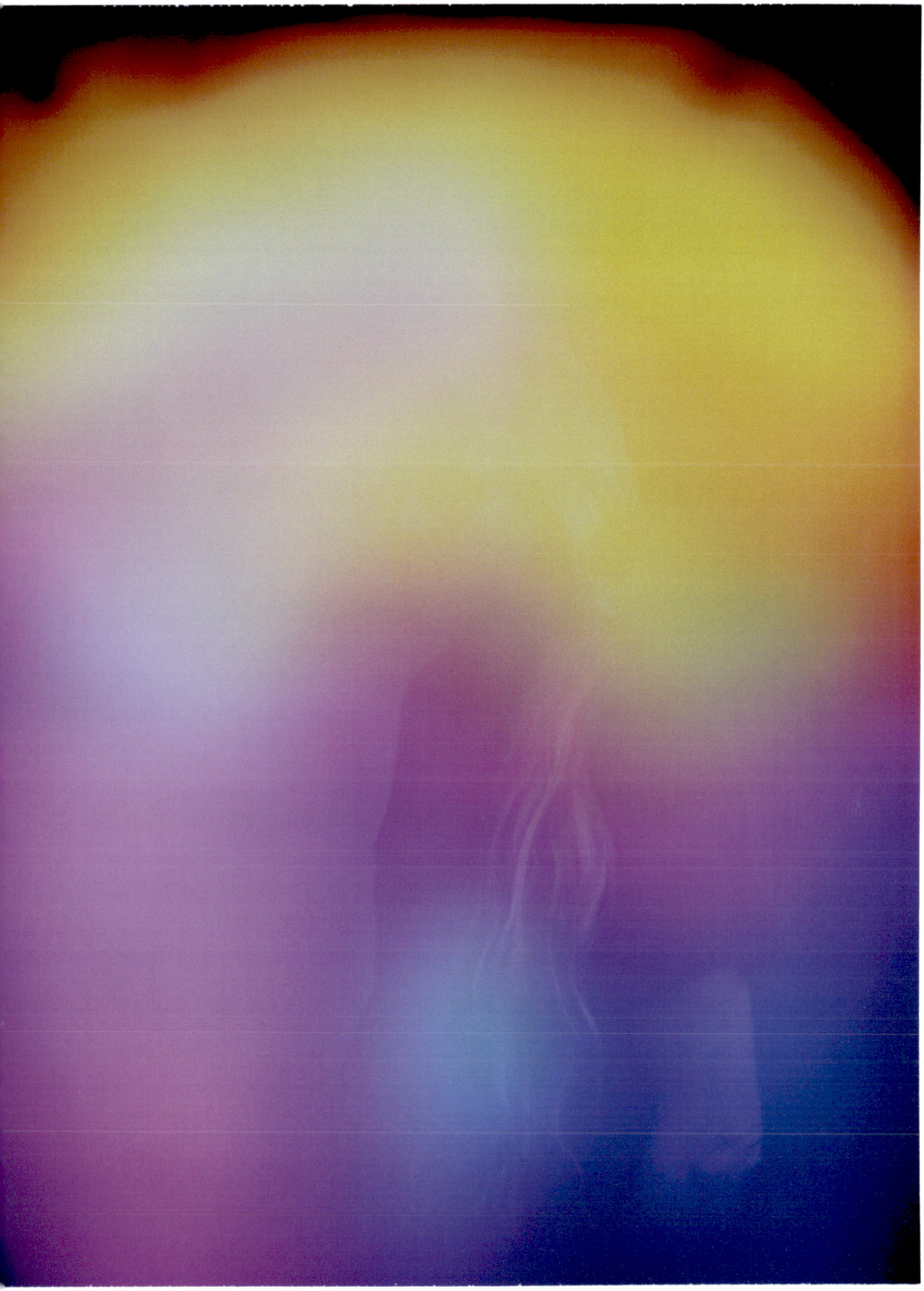

CENTER
GREEN
Healing, Teaching

```
            *G*
       *G*        *G*
     *G*   .***.   *G*
    *G*   * @ @ *   *G*
    *G*   *  ,  *   *G*
    *G*   *( v )*   *G*
    *G*    *   *    *G*
   *G*   .**   **.   *G*
  *G*   *           *   *G*
 *G*   *  .*     *.  *   *G*
 *G*   *  .  *  *  .  *   *G*
 *G*   *  .  *  *  .  *   *G*
 *G*   *  .   * *   .  *   *G*
 *G*   *  .  *  *  .  *   *G*
 *G*   *  .*     *.  *   *G*
 *G*   *  .*     *.  *   *G*
       *. *     * .*
       *..       ..*
```

RIGHT　　　　LEFT

GREEN　　　　GREEN

Healing, Teaching　　　　Healing, Teaching

CENTER (EXPERIENCE) Color above subjects head.
Indicates what the subject is experiencing. It is the color that would best describe them.
--Healing, elasticity of will-- would best describe you. Green is perseverance and tenacity. Persistence, self-assertion, obstinacy self-esteem, and teaching are the qualities most important to you.

RIGHT SIDE (EXPRESSION) Color on subjects right.
Indicates the personality that the subject projects outward and how other people see them.
Healing energy being expressed. An expression of firmness, of constancy, and resistance to change.
--Elastic tension--. Possession is regarded as increasing both security and self esteem.
The person putting out this vibration is willing to work, to gain wealth in terms of educational, cultural, or physical attainments.

LEFT SIDE (FUTURE) Color on subjects left.
Indicates what the subject is creating for themself in the near future.
Green is a growth color, it brings spring to mind. Like the new grass popping up out of the dark soil, small leaves stretching out from the barren branch-ends, as the last days of winter slumber fade and the renewal of life begins. Your future will be a growing time, a time for renewal, life springs forth. You are bringing in the healing energy to your life.

Richard Kern, 2010.

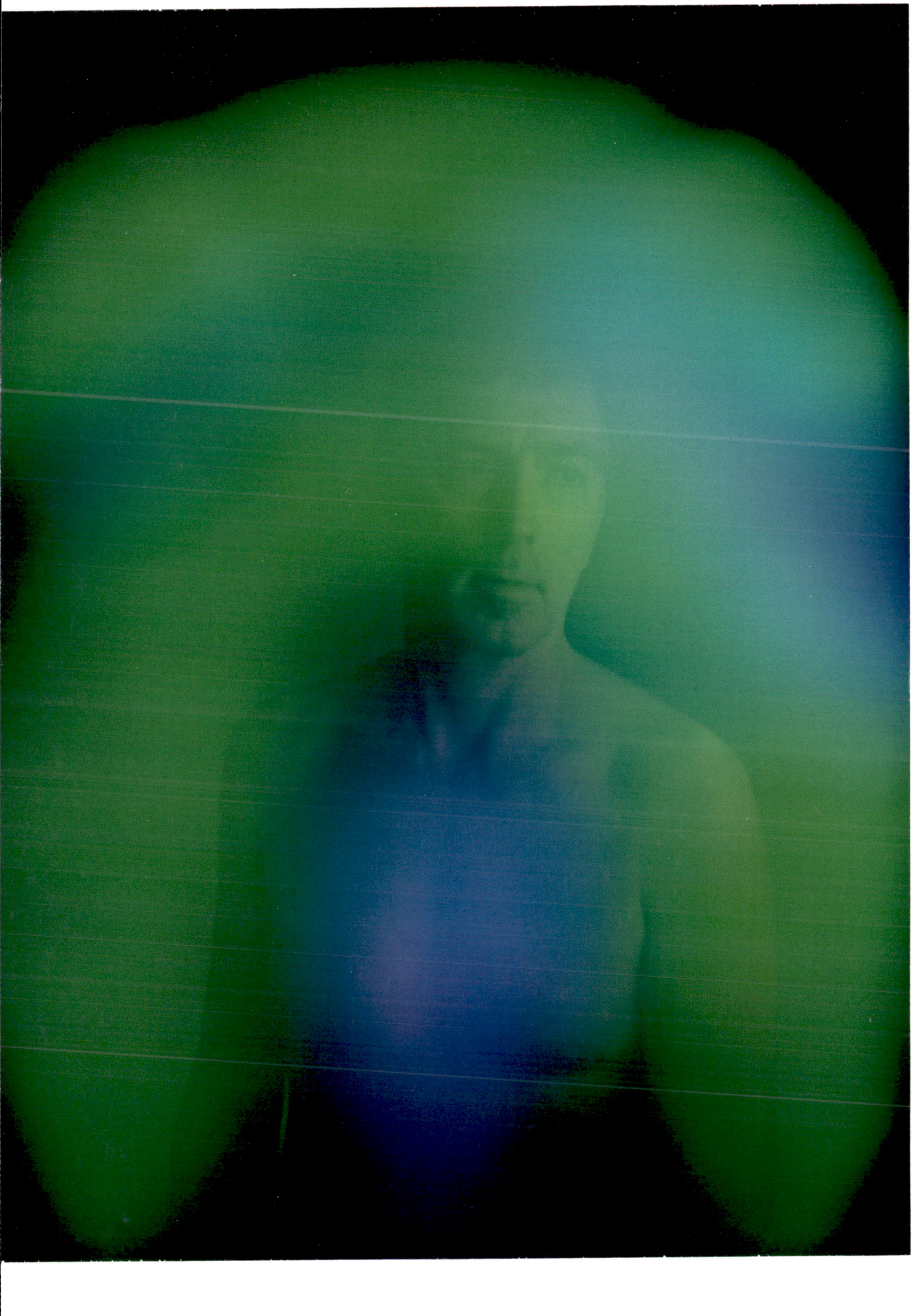

CENTER
WHITE
Spiritually Motivated

```
                *W*
           *W*         *W*
       *W*    .***.    *W*
     *W*    * @ @ *     *W*
     *W*    *  ,  *     *W*
     *W*    *( v )*     *W*
     *W*     *   *      *W*
   *V*     .**   **.     *V*
  *V*     *         *     *V*
*V*     *  .*      *.  *     *V*
*V*     *  .  *   *  .  *    *V*
*V*     *  .  *   *  .  *    *V*
*V*     *  .   * *   .  *    *V*
*V*     *  .  *   *  .  *    *V*
*V*     *  .*      *.  *     *V*
*V*     *  .*      *.  *     *V*
        *.  *      *  .*
        *..          ..*
```

RIGHT — VIOLET — Mystical, Unifying

LEFT — VIOLET — Mystical, Unifying

**CENTER** (EXPERIENCE) Color above subjects head.
Indicates what the subject is experiencing. It is the color that would best describe them.
--Spiritually motivated-- would best describe you. White has the qualities of all of the colors.

**RIGHT SIDE** (EXPRESSION) Color on subjects right.
Indicates the personality that the subject projects outward and how other people see them.
People see you as magical. You put out the highest vibrational frequency. What you want comes to you as if by magic. You seem to get everything you need. A mystic union, a high degree of sensitive intimacy, leading to complete fusion between you and what you put your attention on.

**LEFT SIDE** (FUTURE) Color on subjects left.
Indicates what the subject is creating for themself in the near future.
Spiritual evolution is in store for you. Violet is a mix of blue --unlimited knowledge-- and red --activity--. Therefore spiritual activity will be in your aura. Violet brings unlimited knowledge. You will encounter the rays of guide energies, the highest vibrational frequencies will be distributed to you.

Jun Nakayama, 2009.

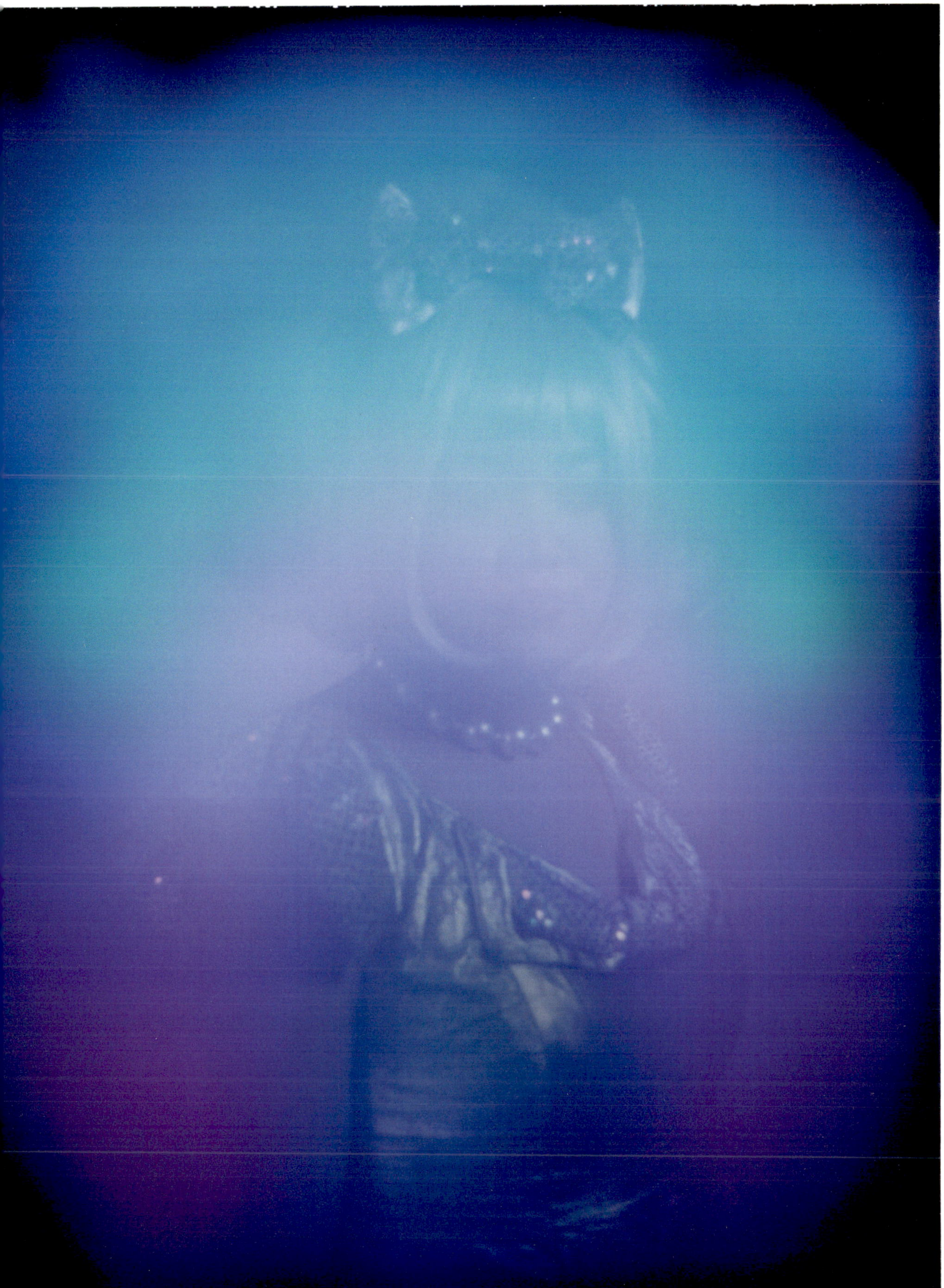

CENTER
RED
Force of Will

```
          *R*
      *R*     *R*
    *R*  .***.  *R*
   *R*  * @ @ *  *R*
   *R*  *  ,  *  *R*
   *R*  *( v )*  *R*
   *R*   *   *   *R*
  *R*  .**   **.  *R*
 *R*  *         *  *R*
*R*  * .*     *. *  *R*
*R*  * . *   * . *  *R*
*R*  * . *   * . *  *R*
*R*  * .  * *  . *  *R*
*R*  * . *   * . *  *R*
*R*  * .*     *. *  *R*
*R*  * .*     *. *  *R*
     *. *     * .*
     *..       ..*
```

RIGHT LEFT

RED RED

Force of Will Force of Will

**CENTER** (EXPERIENCE) Color above subjects head.
Indicates what the subject is experiencing. It is the color that would best describe them.
--Force of will, passion-- would best describe you. Red is the urge to achieve results, to be successful. It is to hungrily desire all those things which offer intensity of living and fullness of experience. Desire, excitability, domination, and passion are the qualities most important to you.

**RIGHT SIDE** (EXPRESSION) Color on subjects right.
Indicates the personality that the subject projects outward and how other people see them.
You work hard at whatever you do. Intensity of experience and fullness of living. Conquest, energy-expanding, you put the energy out. The world sees you as alive, outgoing, sexual, and powerful.

**LEFT SIDE** (FUTURE) Color on subjects left.
Indicates what the subject is creating for themself in the near future.
Stop lights, warning lights, pushing the limits -- these things may have something in common with your future. Life in the fast lane. A time to experience life to its fullest. Stimulating activity, pick up circulation, get going. Your future is full of energy. Doing things, accomplishment, a time to start projects or finish them. Fun is ahead for you.

Dakota Goldhor, 2010.

CENTER
YELLOW
Sunny, Exhilaration

```
          *Y*
      *Y*     *Y*
    *Y*  .***.  *Y*
   *Y*  * @ @ *  *Y*
   *Y*  *  ,  *  *Y*
   *Y*  *( v )*  *Y*
   *Y*   *   *   *Y*
  *Y*  .**   **.  *Y*
 *Y*  *         *  *Y*
*Y*  * .*     *. *  *Y*
*Y*  * . *   * . *  *Y*
*Y*  * . *   * . *  *Y*
*Y*  * .  * *  . *  *Y*
*Y*  * . *   * . *  *Y*
*Y*  * .*     *. *  *Y*
*Y*  * .*     *. *  *Y*
     *. *     * .*
     *..       ..*
```

RIGHT

YELLOW

Sunny, Exhilaration

LEFT

YELLOW

Sunny, Exhilaration

**CENTER** (EXPERIENCE) Color above subjects head.
**Indicates what the subject is experiencing. It is the color that would best describe them.**
Yellow corresponds symbolically to the welcome warmth of sunlight. Variability, expectancy, originality, smiling, and exhilaration are the qualities most important to you.

**RIGHT SIDE** (EXPRESSION) Color on subjects right.
**Indicates the personality that the subject projects outward and how other people see them.**
The world sees you as cheerful. Gold is the brightest color. You may find yourself the center of attention, with others revolving around you. Radiant, and expansive. You represent relaxation, a release from burdens, problems, harassment or restriction. Your energy shines from you like the warmth of the sun, giving happiness and joy to all who stand in the radiance of your smile, and you do smile a lot.

**LEFT SIDE** (FUTURE) Color on Subjects left.
**Indicates what the subject is creating for themself in the near future.**
Your future is bound to be thought provoking. Like the rising sun, yellow brings warmth. Yellows are representative of the intellect. Each shade or tint of yellow expresses a type of function, ability, or expression of the intellect, from the craftiness of a mustard yellow, to the high thought of golden yellow. You approach the future with a sense of excitement and joy.

Sara Rossein, 2009.

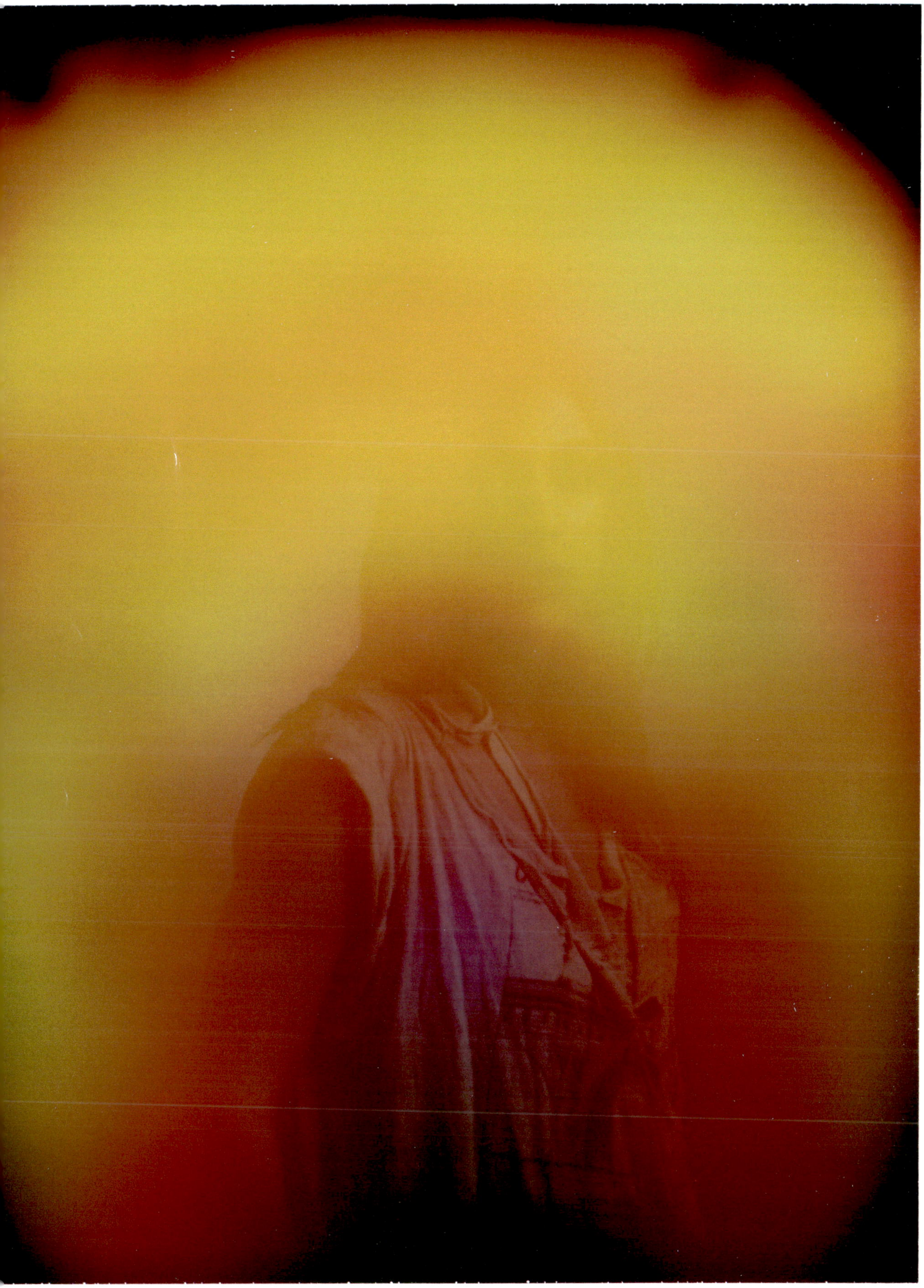

```
               CENTER
                 RED
            Force of Will

                  *R*
              *R*     *R*
            *R*  .***.  *R*
           *R*  * @ @ *  *R*
           *R*  *  ,  *  *R*
           *R*  *( v )*  *R*
           *R*   *   *   *R*
          *R*  .**   **.  *O*
         *R*  *         *  *O*
        *R*  * .*     *. *  *O*
        *R*  * . *   * . *  *O*
        *R*  * . *   * . *  *O*
        *R*  * .  * *  . *  *O*
        *R*  * . *   * . *  *O*
        *R*  * .*     *. *  *O*
        *R*  * .*     *. *  *O*
             *. *     * .*
             *..       ..*

         RIGHT              LEFT

         RED                ORANGE
```

Force of Will

Creative, Artistic

**CENTER** (EXPERIENCE) Color above subjects head.
Indicates what the subject is experiencing. It is the color that would best describe them.
--Force of will, passion-- would best describe you. Red is the urge to achieve results, to be successful. It is to hungrily desire all those things which offer intensity of living and fullness of experience. Desire, excitability, domination, and passion are the qualities most important to you.

**RIGHT SIDE** (EXPRESSION) Color on subjects right.
Indicates the personality that the subject projects outward and how other people see them.
You work hard at whatever you do. Intensity of experience and fullness of living. Conquest, energy-expanding, you put the energy out. The world sees you as alive, outgoing, sexual, and powerful.

**LEFT SIDE** (FUTURE) Color on Subjects left.
Indicates what the subject is creating for themself in the near future.
Activity generating energy is coming into your field. Orange is a mixture of active red and intellectual yellow, making a very creative future for you. Activity, wakefulness, and creativity unfolding. An opportunity to enjoy the sensual pleasures. Orange is known to give way to green, healing and growth, after the balancing period is over. Now is the time to go for it.

Tim Barber (Two), 2009.

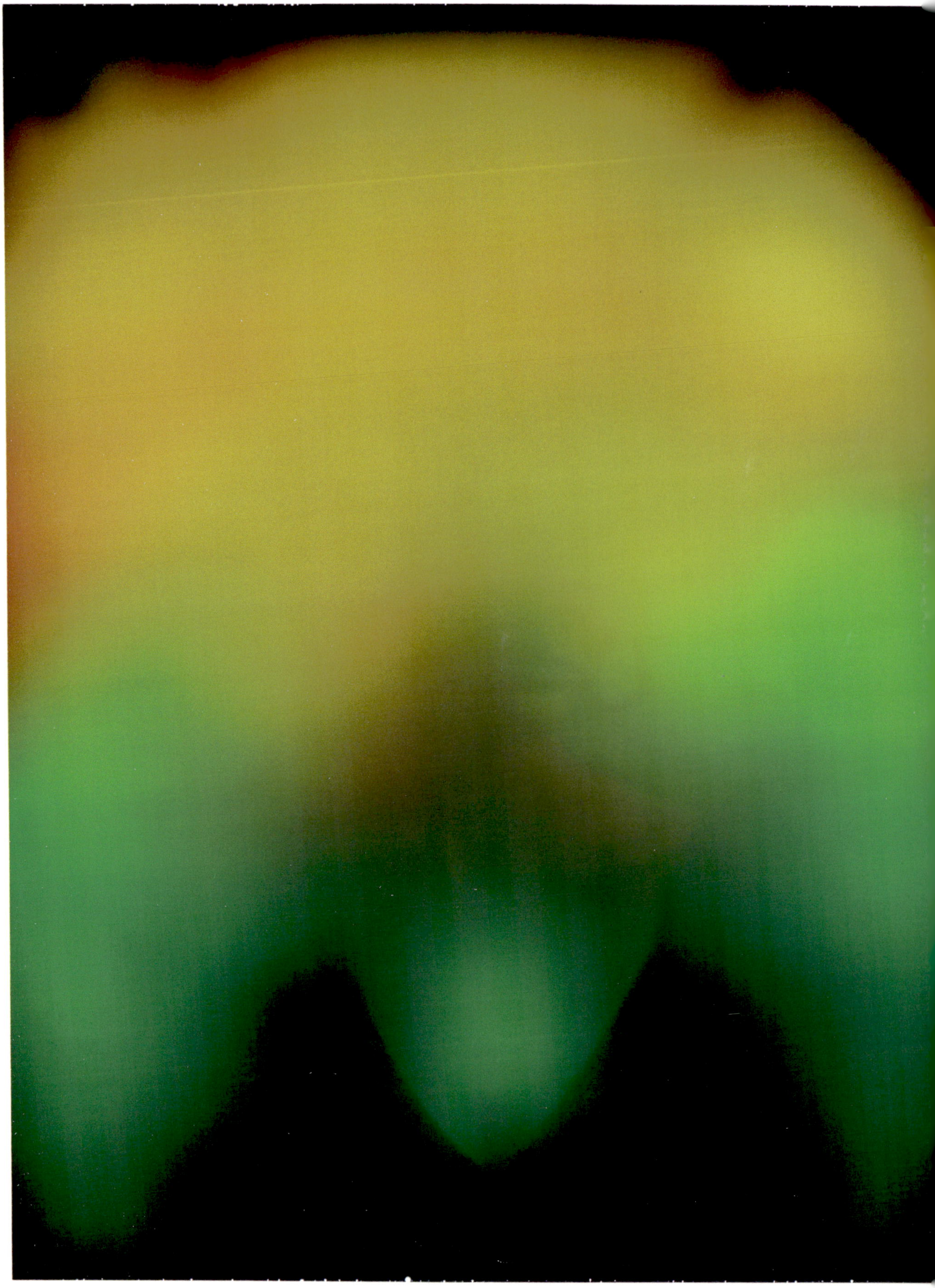

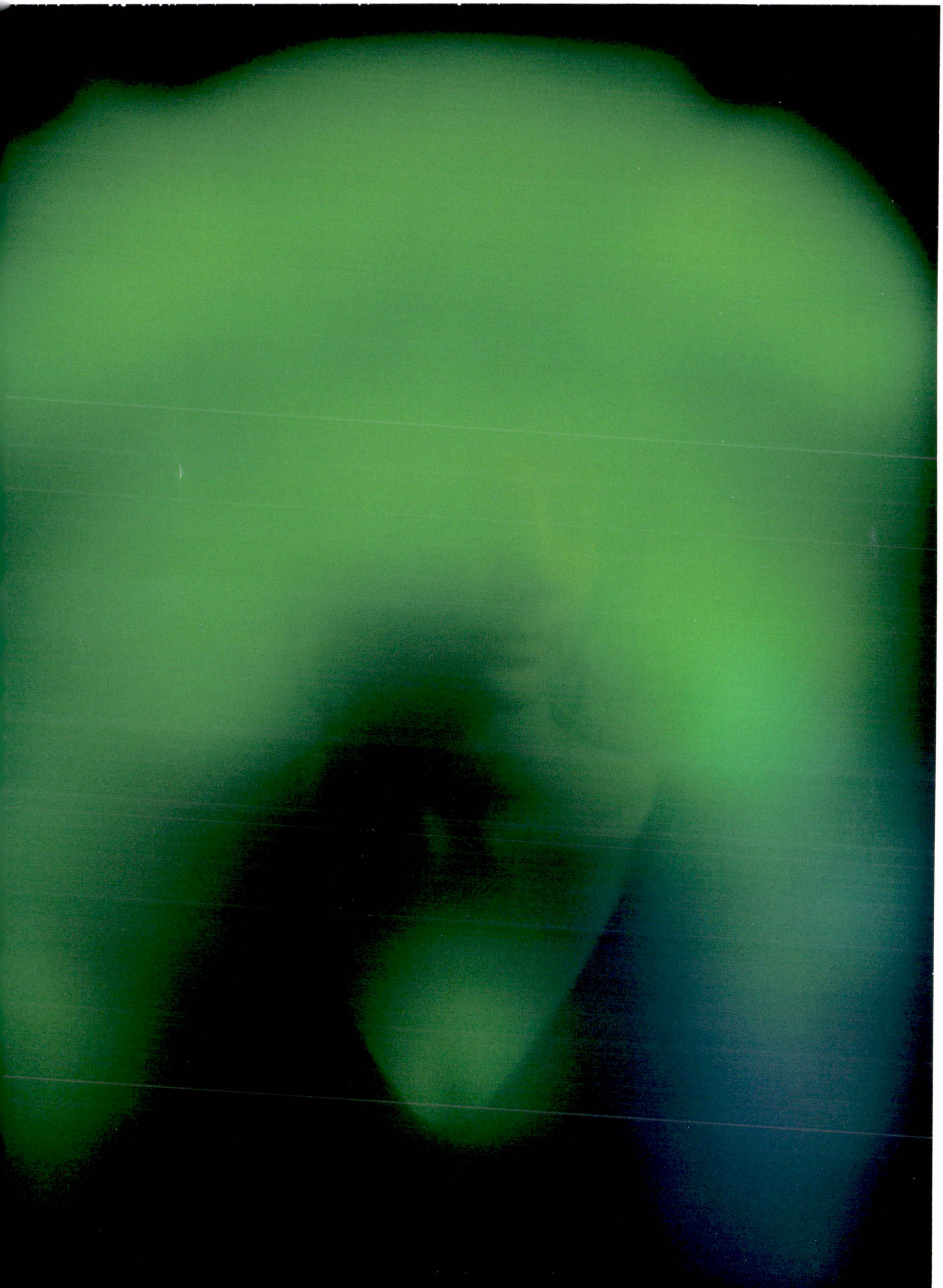

CENTER
YELLOW
Sunny, Exhilaration

```
          *Y*
     *Y*      *Y*
   *Y*  .***.   *Y*
  *Y*  * @ @ *   *Y*
  *Y*  *  ,  *   *Y*
  *Y*  *( v )*   *Y*
  *Y*   *   *    *Y*
 *G*   .**   **.  *G*
*G*   *         *   *G*
*G*   * .*    *. *   *G*
*G*   * . *  * . *   *G*
*G*   * . *  * . *   *G*
*G*   * .  * *  . *  *G*
*G*   * . *  * . *   *G*
*G*   * .*    *. *   *G*
*G*   * .*    *. *   *G*
      *. *    * .*
      *..      ..*
```

RIGHT GREEN Healing, Teaching

LEFT GREEN Healing, Teaching

**CENTER** (EXPERIENCE) Color above subjects head.
Indicates what the subject is experiencing. It is the color that would best describe them.
Yellow corresponds symbolically to the welcome warmth of sunlight. Variability, expectancy, originality, smiling,and exhilaration are the qualities most important to you.

**RIGHT SIDE** (EXPRESSION) Color on subjects right.
Indicates the personality that the subject projects outward and how other people see them.
Healing energy being expressed. An expression of firmness, of constancy, and resistance to change. --Elastic tension--. Possession is regarded as increasing both security and self esteem.
The person putting out this vibration is willing to work, to gain wealth in terms of educational, cultural, or physical attainments.

**LEFT SIDE** (FUTURE) Color on subjects left.
Indicates what the subject is creating for themself in the near future.
Green is a growth color, it brings spring to mind. Like the new grass popping up out of the dark soil, small leaves stretching out from the barren branch-ends, as the last days of winter slumber fade and the renewal of life begins. Your future will be a growing time, a time for renewal, life springs forth. You are bringing in the healing energy to your life.

Maris Bellack (One), 2011.

```
               CENTER
                GREEN
        Healing, Teaching

          *G*
      *G*       *G*
    *G*   .***.   *G*
   *G*   * @ @ *   *G*
   *G*   *  ,  *   *G*
   *G*   *( v )*   *G*
   *G*    *   *    *G*
  *G*   .**   **.   *G*
 *G*   *         *   *G*
*G*   * .*     *. *   *G*
*G*   * . *   * . *   *G*
*G*   * . *   * . *   *G*
*G*   * .  * *  . *   *G*
*G*   * . *   * . *   *G*
*G*   * .*     *. *   *G*
*G*   * .*     *. *   *G*
      *. *     * .*
      *..       ..*

 RIGHT               LEFT

 GREEN               GREEN

Healing, Teaching                    Healing, Teaching
```

**CENTER** (EXPERIENCE) Color above subjects head.
**Indicates what the subject is experiencing. It is the color that would best describe them.**
--Healing, elasticity of will-- would best describe you. Green is perseverance and tenacity. Persistence, self-assertion, obstinacy self-esteem, and teaching are the qualities most important to you.

**RIGHT SIDE** (EXPRESSION) Color on subjects right.
**Indicates the personality that the subject projects outward and how other people see them.**
Healing energy being expressed. An expression of firmness, of constancy, and resistance to change.
--Elastic tension--. Possession is regarded as increasing both security and self esteem.
The person putting out this vibration is willing to work, to gain wealth in terms of educational, cultural, or physical attainments.

**LEFT SIDE** (FUTURE) Color on subjects left.
**Indicates what the subject is creating for themself in the near future.**
Green is a growth color, it brings spring to mind. Like the new grass popping up out of the dark soil, small leaves stretching out from the barren branch-ends, as the last days of winter slumber fade and the renewal of life begins. Your future will be a growing time, a time for renewal, life springs forth. You are bringing in the healing energy to your life.

Maris Bellack (Two), 2011.

```
             CENTER
             ORANGE
       Creative, Artistic

               *O*
           *O*     *O*
         *O*  .***.  *O*
        *O*  * @ @ *  *O*
        *O*  *  ,  *  *O*
        *O*  *( v )*  *O*
        *O*   *   *   *O*
       *V*  .**   **.  *B*
      *V*  *         *  *B*
     *V*  * .*     *. *  *B*
     *V*  * . *   * . *  *B*
     *V*  * . *   * . *  *B*
     *V*  * .  * *  . *  *B*
     *V*  * . *   * . *  *B*
     *V*  * .*     *. *  *B*
     *V*  * .*     *. *  *B*
          *. *     * .*
          *..       ..*

      RIGHT              LEFT

      VIOLET             BLUE

Mystical, Unifying            Peaceful, Contemplative
```

**CENTER** (EXPERIENCE) Color above subjects head.
Indicates what the subject is experiencing. It is the color that would best describe them.
--Creative, artistic-- would best describe you. Orange represents energy with mental direction. You are alive, artistic, perceptive creative. Constructive self expression is important to you.

**RIGHT SIDE** (EXPRESSION) Color on subjects right.
Indicates the personality that the subject projects outward and how other people see them.
People see you as magical. You put out the highest vibrational frequency. What you want comes to you as if by magic. You seem to get everything you need. A mystic union, a high degree of sensitive intimacy, leading to complete fusion between you and what you put your attention on.

**LEFT SIDE** (FUTURE) Color on subjects left.
Indicates what the subject is creating for themself in the near future.
Blue is a communication color, so you are a good listener, an intuitive listener, able to transform others through loving listening. It may be a good time to learn. You can be fairly certain when studying or learning on whatever level. If it is a ray or guiding light, you are being stimulated to learn about something which is important to your evolution. Peaceful times are in your future.

Michael Nevin, 2008.

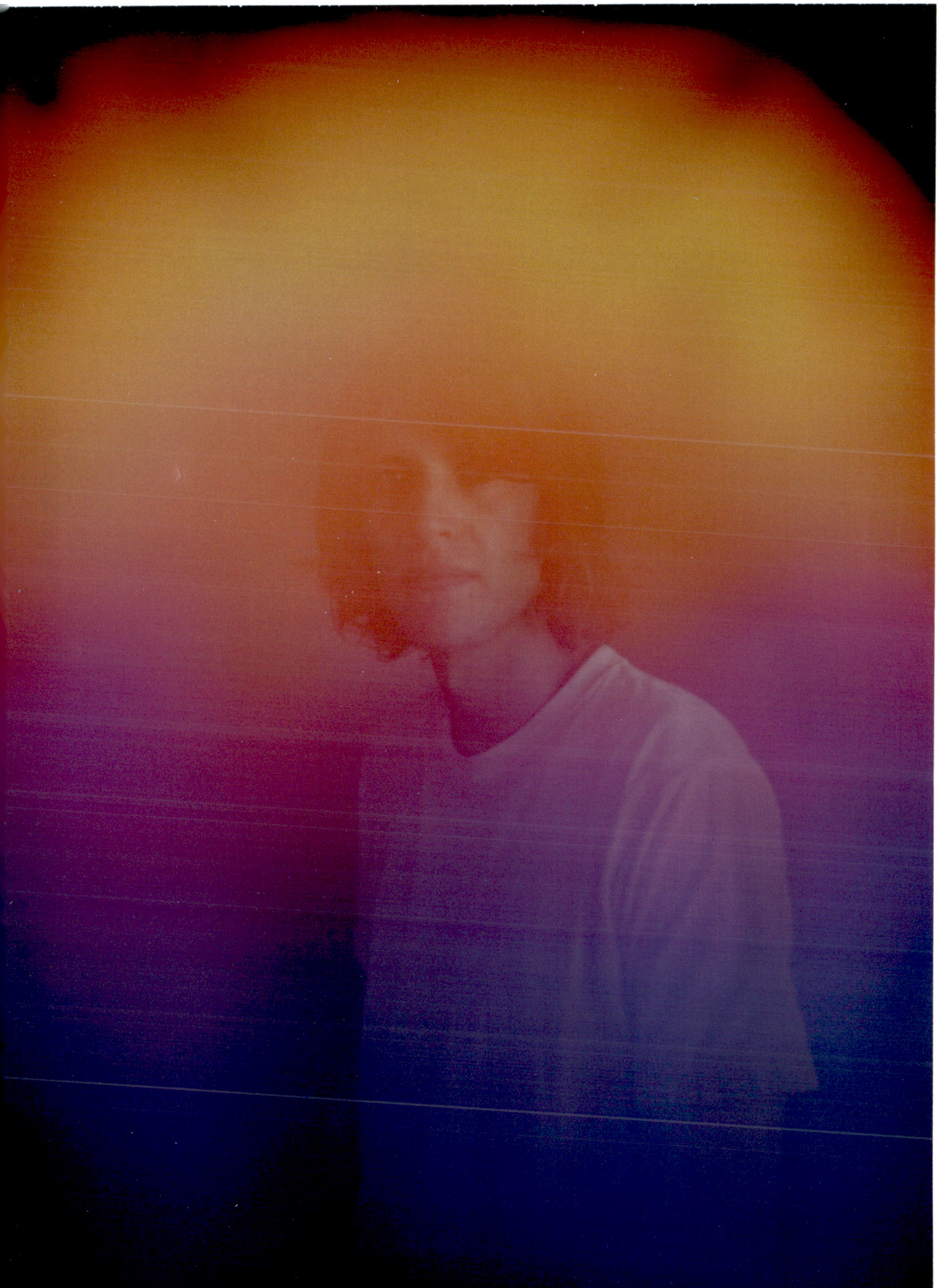

```
        CENTER
        VIOLET
   Mystical, Unifying

          *V*
      *V*     *V*
    *V*  .***.  *V*
   *V*  * @ @ *  *V*
   *V*  *  ,  *  *V*
   *V*  *( v )*  *V*
   *V*   *   *   *V*
  *V*  .**   **.  *V*
 *V*  *         *  *V*
*V*  * .*     *. *  *V*
*V*  * . *   * . *  *V*
*V*  * . *   * . *  *V*
*V*  * .  * *  . *  *V*
*V*  * . *   * . *  *V*
*V*  * .*     *. *  *V*
*V*  * .*     *. *  *V*
     *. *     * .*
     *..       ..*
```

RIGHT

VIOLET

Mystical, Unifying

LEFT

VIOLET

Mystical, Unifying

**CENTER** (EXPERIENCE) Color above subjects head.
Indicates what the subject is experiencing. It is the color that would best describe them.
--Mystical unifying-- would best describe you. Violet is a high degree of sensitive intimacy, leading to complete fusion between subject and object, so that everything which is thought and desired must become reality. Enchantment, charm, sensitivity and deep spiritual understanding are the qualities most important to you.

**RIGHT SIDE** (EXPRESSION) Color on subjects right.
Indicates the personality that the subject projects outward and how other people see them.
People see you as magical. You put out the highest vibrational frequency. What you want comes to you as if by magic. You seem to get everything you need. A mystic union, a high degree of sensitive intimacy, leading to complete fusion between you and what you put your attention on.

**LEFT SIDE** (FUTURE) Color on subjects left.
Indicates what the subject is creating for themself in the near future.
Spiritual evolution is in store for you. Violet is a mix of blue --unlimited knowledge-- and red --activity--. Therefore spiritual activity will be in your aura. Violet brings unlimited knowledge. You will encounter the rays of guide energies, the highest vibrational frequencies will be distributed to you.

Cesar Llacuna, 2010.

CENTER
ORANGE
Creative, Artistic

```
          *O*
      *O*     *O*
    *O*  .***.  *O*
   *O*  * @ @ *  *O*
   *O*  *  ,  *  *O*
   *O*  *( v )*  *O*
   *O*   *   *   *O*
  *R*  .**   **.  *O*
 *R*  *         *  *O*
*R*  * .*     *. *  *O*
*R*  * . *   * . *  *O*
*R*  * . *   * . *  *O*
*R*  * .  * *  . *  *O*
*R*  * . *   * . *  *O*
*R*  * .*     *. *  *O*
*R*  * .*     *. *  *O*
     *. *     * .*
     *..       ..*
```

RIGHT | LEFT
RED | ORANGE
Force of Will | Creative, Artistic

**CENTER** (EXPERIENCE) Color above subjects head.
Indicates what the subject is experiencing. It is the color that would best describe them.
--Creative, artistic-- would best describe you. Orange represents energy with mental direction. You are alive, artistic, perceptive creative. Constructive self expression is important to you.

**RIGHT SIDE** (EXPRESSION) Color on subjects right.
Indicates the personality that the subject projects outward and how other people see them.
You work hard at whatever you do. Intensity of experience and fullness of living. Conquest, energy-expanding, you put the energy out. The world sees you as alive, outgoing, sexual, and powerful.

**LEFT SIDE** (FUTURE) Color on subjects left.
Indicates what the subject is creating for themself in the near future.
Activity generating energy is coming into your field. Orange is a mixture of active red and intellectual yellow, making a very creative future for you. Activity, wakefulness, and creativity unfolding. An opportunity to enjoy the sensual pleasures. Orange is known to give way to green, healing and growth, after the balancing period is over. Now is the time to go for it.

Beverly Van de Roer, 2010.

CENTER
WHITE
Spiritually Motivated

```
               *W*
          *W*       *W*
        *W*   .***.   *W*
       *W*   * @ @ *   *W*
       *W*   *  ,  *   *W*
       *W*   *( v )*   *W*
       *W*    *   *    *W*
      *W*   .**   **.   *W*
    *W*   *           *   *W*
   *W*   * .*       *. *   *W*
   *W*   * . *     * . *   *W*
   *W*   * . *     * . *   *W*
   *W*   * .  * *  . *   *W*
   *W*   * . *     * . *   *W*
   *W*   * .*       *. *   *W*
   *W*   * .*       *. *   *W*
         *. *       * .*
         *..         ..*
```

RIGHT                LEFT

WHITE                WHITE

Spiritually Motivated                Spiritually Motivated

**CENTER** (EXPERIENCE) Color above subjects head.
**Indicates what the subject is experiencing. It is the color that would best describe them.**
--Spiritually motivated-- would best describe you. White has the qualities of all of the colors.

**RIGHT SIDE** (EXPRESSION) Color on subjects right.
**Indicates the personality that the subject projects outward and how other people see them.**
You have a healing effect on all in your field. White is a mixture of all the colors. You emit all the qualities at the same time. Though white tends to be unstable, like a supernova, it is a healing experience. You could be a spiritual leader.

**LEFT SIDE** (FUTURE) Color on subjects left.
**Indicates what the subject is creating for themself in the near future.**
Very bright. A healing is coming for you and those around you. You are not a novice as the beauty of white light attracts all beings at every level of existence. These beings are very loving. They are there to help your evolution, a time to assist others in transition, or to make transitions yourself.

Betty Ralph (Four), 2010.

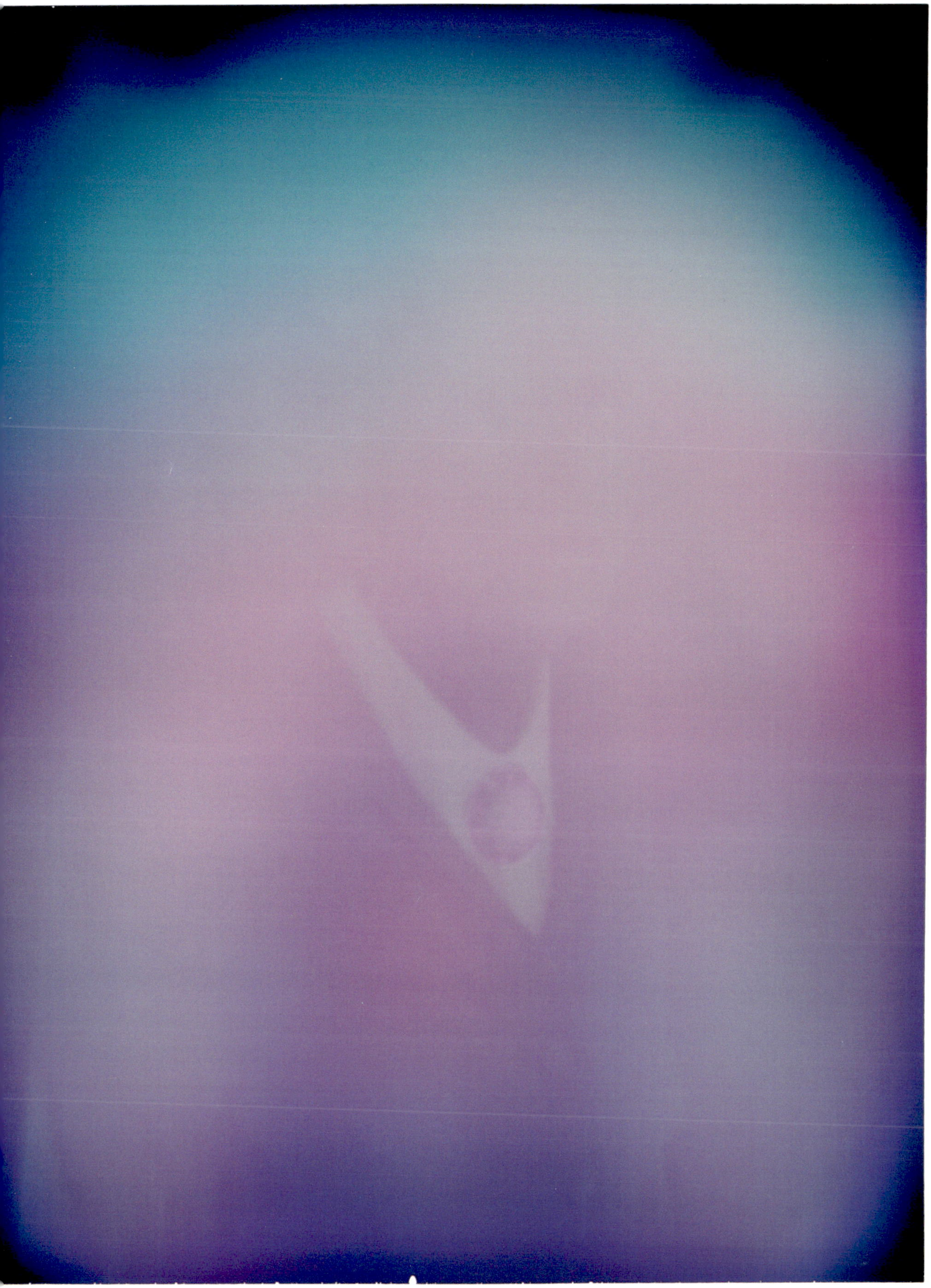

CENTER
BLUE
Peaceful, Contemplative

```
          *B*
      *B*     *B*
    *B*  .***.  *B*
   *B*  * @ @ *  *B*
   *B*  *  ,  *  *B*
   *B*  *( v )*  *B*
   *B*   *   *   *B*
  *G*  .**   **.  *B*
 *G*  *         *  *B*
*G*  * .*     *. *  *B*
*G*  * . *   * . *  *B*
*G*  * . *   * . *  *B*
*G*  * .  * *  . *  *B*
*G*  * . *   * . *  *B*
*G*  * .*     *. *  *B*
*G*  * .*     *. *  *B*
     *. *     * .*
     *..       ..*
```

RIGHT — GREEN — Healing, Teaching

LEFT — BLUE — Peaceful, Contemplative

**CENTER** (EXPERIENCE) Color above subjects head.
**Indicates what the subject is experiencing. It is the color that would best describe them.**
--Depth of feeling-- would best describe you. Blue is the blissful fulfillment of the highest ideals of unity, of at-one-ness, of a reunion with earth-mother. It is truth and trust, love and dedication. Peace, tranquility, contentment, tenderness, love, and affection are the qualities most important to you.

**RIGHT SIDE** (EXPRESSION) Color on subjects right.
**Indicates the personality that the subject projects outward and how other people see them.**
Healing energy being expressed. An expression of firmness, of constancy, and resistance to change. --Elastic tension--. Possession is regarded as increasing both security and self esteem. The person putting out this vibration is willing to work, to gain wealth in terms of educational, cultural, or physical attainments.

**LEFT SIDE** (FUTURE) Color on subjects left.
**Indicates what the subject is creating for themself in the near future.**
Blue is a communication color, so you are a good listener, an intuitive listener, able to transform others through loving listening. It may be a good time to learn. You can be fairly certain when studying or learning on whatever level. If it is a ray or guiding light, you are being stimulated to learn about something which is important to your evolution. Peaceful times are in your future.

Madeleine Von Froomer, 2009.

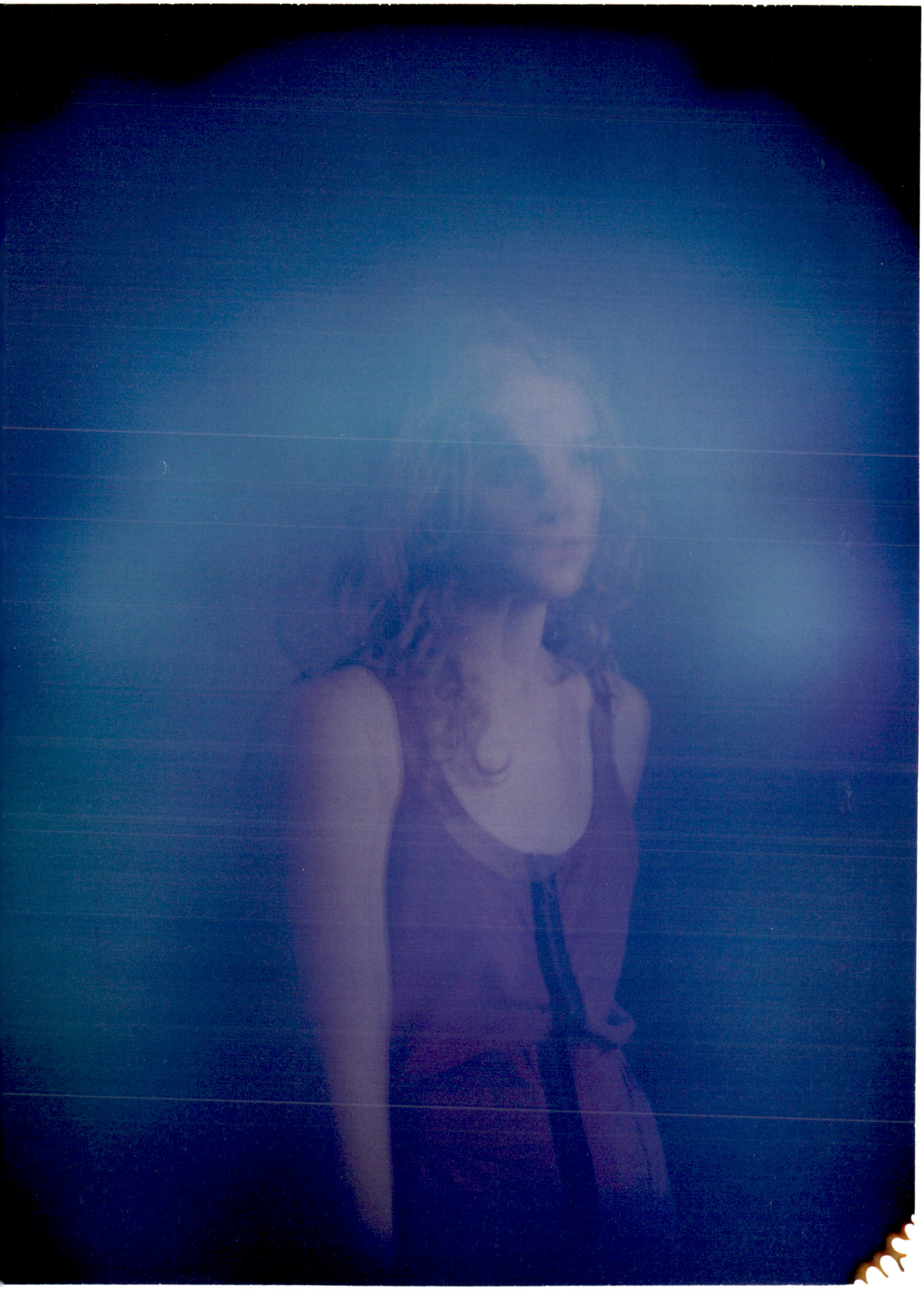

CENTER
ORANGE
Creative, Artistic

```
          *O*
      *O*     *O*
    *O*  .***.  *O*
   *O*  * @ @ *  *O*
   *O*  *  ,  *  *O*
   *O*  *( v )*  *O*
   *O*   *   *   *O*
  *R*  .**   **.  *G*
 *R*  *         *  *G*
*R*  * .*     *. *  *G*
*R*  * . *   * . *  *G*
*R*  * . *   * . *  *G*
*R*  * .  * *  . *  *G*
*R*  * . *   * . *  *G*
*R*  * .*     *. *  *G*
*R*  * .*     *. *  *G*
     *. *     * .*
     *..       ..*
```

RIGHT LEFT

RED GREEN

Force of Will Healing, Teaching

**CENTER** (EXPERIENCE) Color above subjects head.
Indicates what the subject is experiencing. It is the color that would best describe them.
--Creative, artistic-- would best describe you. Orange represents energy with mental direction. You are alive, artistic, perceptive creative. Constructive self expression is important to you.

**RIGHT SIDE** (EXPRESSION) Color on subjects right.
Indicates the personality that the subject projects outward and how other people see them.
You work hard at whatever you do. Intensity of experience and fullness of living. Conquest, energy-expanding, you put the energy out. The world sees you as alive, outgoing, sexual, and powerful.

**LEFT SIDE** (FUTURE) Color on Subjects left.
Indicates what the subject is creating for themself in the near future.
Green is a growth color, it brings spring to mind. Like the new grass popping up out of the dark soil, small leaves stretching out from the barren branch-ends, as the last days of winter slumber fade and the renewal of life begins. Your future will be a growing time, a time for renewal, life springs forth. You are bringing in the healing energy to your life.

Benjamin Morsberger, 2008.

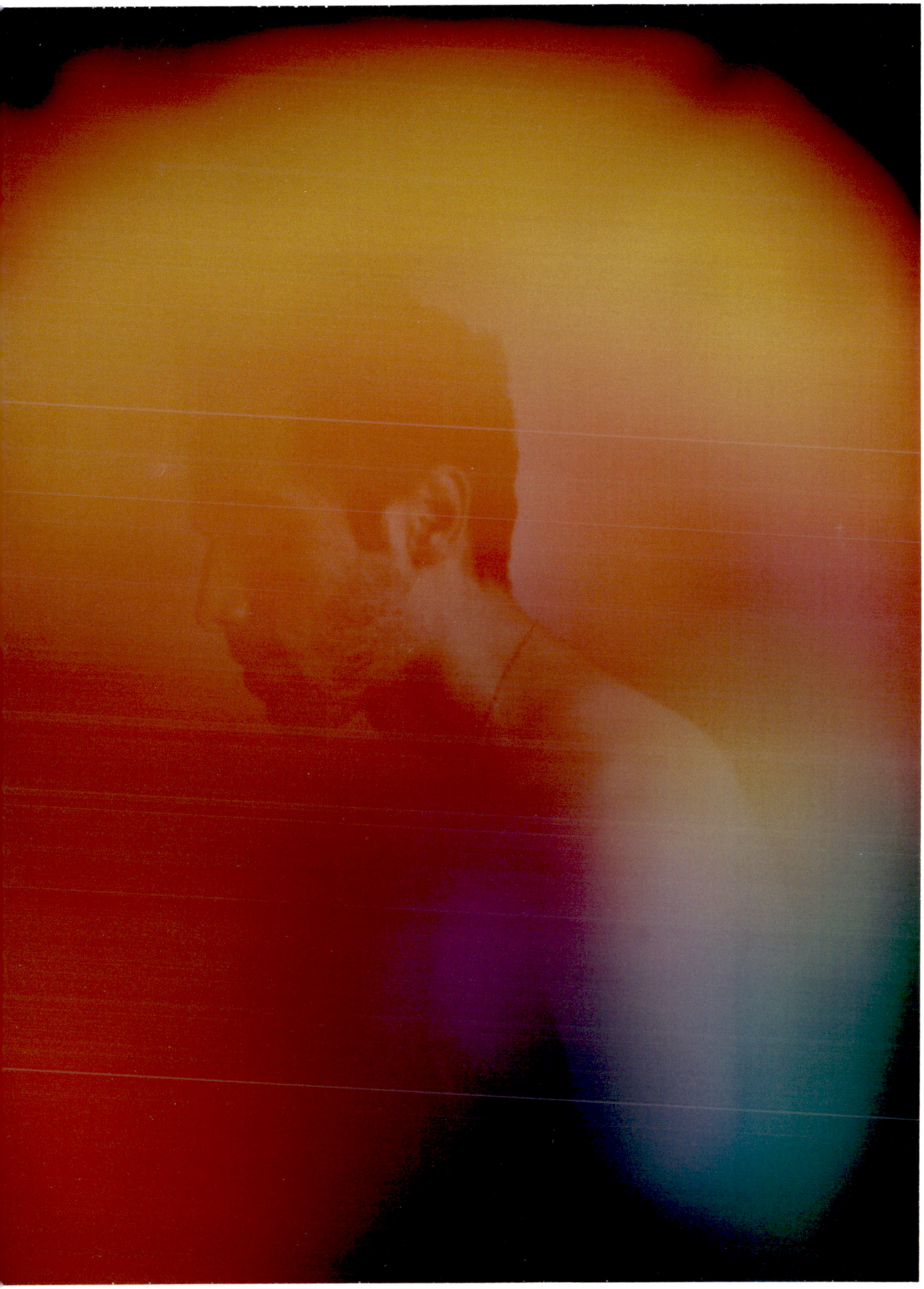

```
              CENTER
               RED
        Force of Will

                *R*
            *R*     *R*
          *R*  .***.  *R*
         *R*  * @ @ *  *R*
         *R*  *  ,  *  *R*
         *R*  *( v )*  *R*
         *R*   *   *   *R*
        *R*   .**   **.  *O*
       *R*   *         *  *O*
      *R*   * .*     *. *  *O*
      *R*   * . *   * . *  *O*
      *R*   * . *   * . *  *O*
      *R*   * .  * *  . *  *O*
      *R*   * . *   * . *  *O*
      *R*   * .*     *. *  *O*
      *R*   * .*     *. *  *O*
            *. *     * .*
            *..       ..*

       RIGHT              LEFT

       RED                ORANGE

Force of Will                 Creative, Artistic
```

**CENTER** (EXPERIENCE) Color above subjects head.
Indicates what the subject is experiencing. It is the color that would best describe them.
--Force of will, passion-- would best describe you. Red is the urge to achieve results, to be successful. It is to hungrily desire all those things which offer intensity of living and fullness of experience. Desire, excitability, domination, and passion are the qualities most important to you.

**RIGHT SIDE** (EXPRESSION) Color on subjects right.
Indicates the personality that the subject projects outward and how other people see them.
You work hard at whatever you do. Intensity of experience and fullness of living. Conquest, energy-expanding, you put the energy out. The world sees you as alive, outgoing, sexual, and powerful.

**LEFT SIDE** (FUTURE) Color on subjects left.
Indicates what the subject is creating for themself in the near future.
Activity generating energy is coming into your field. Orange is a mixture of active red and intellectual yellow, making a very creative future for you. Activity, wakefulness, and creativity unfolding. An opportunity to enjoy the sensual pleasures. Orange is known to give way to green, healing and growth, after the balancing period is over. Now is the time to go for it.

Jordan Hruska, 2008.

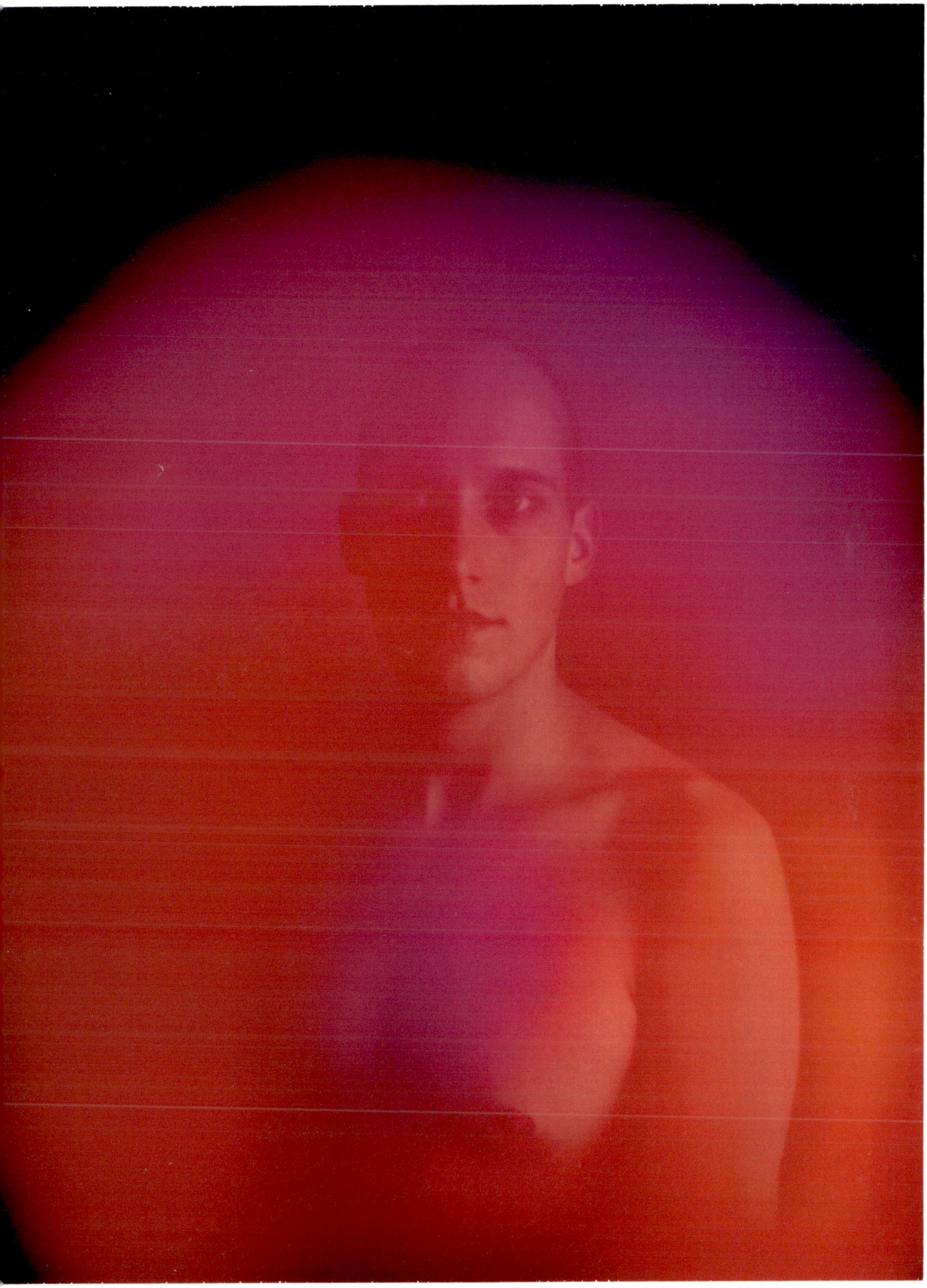

```
          CENTER
          YELLOW
   Sunny, Exhilaration

           *Y*
       *Y*     *Y*
     *Y*  .***.  *Y*
    *Y*  * @ @ *  *Y*
    *Y*  *  ,  *  *Y*
    *Y*  *( v )*  *Y*
    *Y*   *   *   *Y*
   *G*  .**   **.  *B*
  *G*  *         *  *B*
 *G*  * .*     *. *  *B*
 *G*  * . *   * . *  *B*
 *G*  * . *   * . *  *B*
 *G*  * .  * *  . *  *B*
 *G*  * . *   * . *  *B*
 *G*  * .*     *. *  *B*
 *G*  * .*     *. *  *B*
      *. *     * .*
      *..       ..*

  RIGHT              LEFT

  GREEN              BLUE
```

Healing, Teaching

Peaceful, Contemplative

**CENTER** (EXPERIENCE) Color above subjects head.
**Indicates what the subject is experiencing. It is the color that would best describe them.**
Yellow corresponds symbolically to the welcome warmth of sunlight. Variability, expectancy, originality, smiling, and exhilaration are the qualities most important to you.

**RIGHT SIDE** (EXPRESSION) Color on subjects right.
**Indicates the personality that the subject projects outward and how other people see them.**
Healing energy being expressed. An expression of firmness, of constancy, and resistance to change. --Elastic tension--. Possession is regarded as increasing both security and self esteem.
The person putting out this vibration is willing to work, to gain wealth in terms of educational, cultural, or physical attainments.

**LEFT SIDE** (FUTURE) Color on subjects left.
**Indicates what the subject is creating for themself in the near future.**
Blue is a communication color, so you are a good listener, an intuitive listener, able to transform others through loving listening. It may be a good time to learn. You can be fairly certain when studying or learning on whatever level. If it is a ray or guiding light, you are being stimulated to learn about something which is important to your evolution. Peaceful times are in your future.

Bill Powers, 2011.

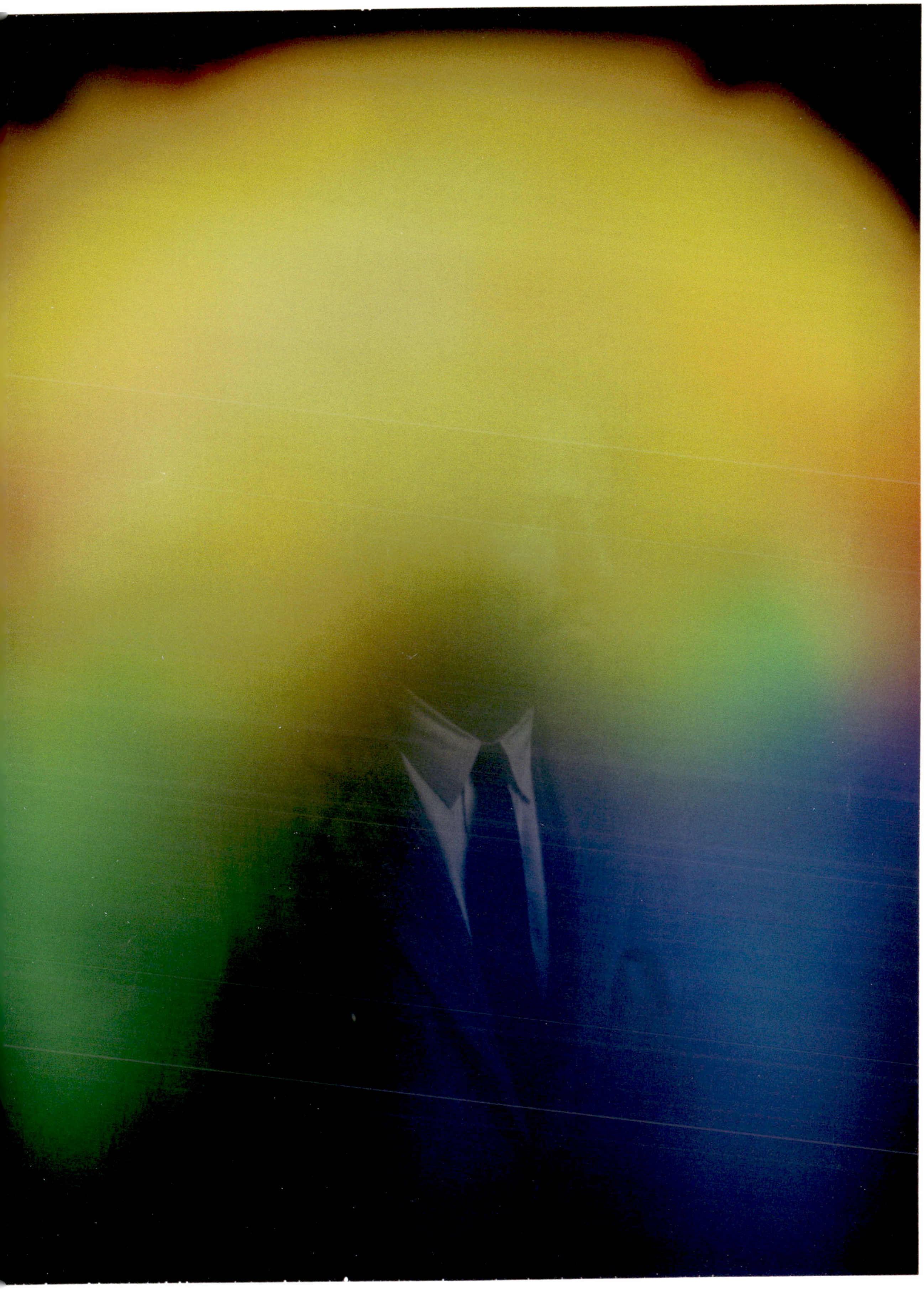

```
          CENTER
           BLUE
  Peaceful, Contemplative

          *B*
      *B*     *B*
    *B*  .***.  *B*
   *B*  * @ @ *  *B*
   *B*  *  ,  *  *B*
   *B*  *( v )*  *B*
   *B*   *   *   *B*
  *B*  .**   **.  *W*
 *B*  *         *  *W*
*B*  * .*     *. *  *W*
*B*  * . *   * . *  *W*
*B*  * . *   * . *  *W*
*B*  * .  * *  . *  *W*
*B*  * . *   * . *  *W*
*B*  * .*     *. *  *W*
*B*  * .*     *. *  *W*
     *. *     * .*
     *..       ..*

 RIGHT            LEFT

 BLUE              WHITE

Peaceful, Contemplative       Spiritually Motivated
```

**CENTER** (EXPERIENCE) Color above subjects head.
**Indicates what the subject is experiencing. It is the color that would best describe them.**
--Depth of feeling-- would best describe you. Blue is the blissful fulfillment of the highest ideals of unity, of at-one-ness, of a reunion with earth-mother. It is truth and trust, love and dedication. Peace, tranquility, contentment, tenderness, love, and affection are the qualities most important to you.

**RIGHT SIDE** (EXPRESSION) Color on subjects right.
**Indicates the personality that the subject projects outward and how other people see them.**
You put calm into the world, contemplation with a pacifying effect. Unification, a sense of belonging. --Blue is loyalty--. Blue corresponds to a depth of feeling. A relaxed sensitivity, empathy for esthetic experience. People see you as the calm of the untroubled sea.

**LEFT SIDE** (FUTURE) Color on subjects left.
**Indicates what the subject is creating for themself in the near future.**
Very bright. A healing is coming for you and those around you. You are not a novice as the beauty of white light attracts all beings at every level of existence. These beings are very loving. They are there to help your evolution, a time to assist others in transition, or to make transitions yourself.

Tashan Barclay, 2011.

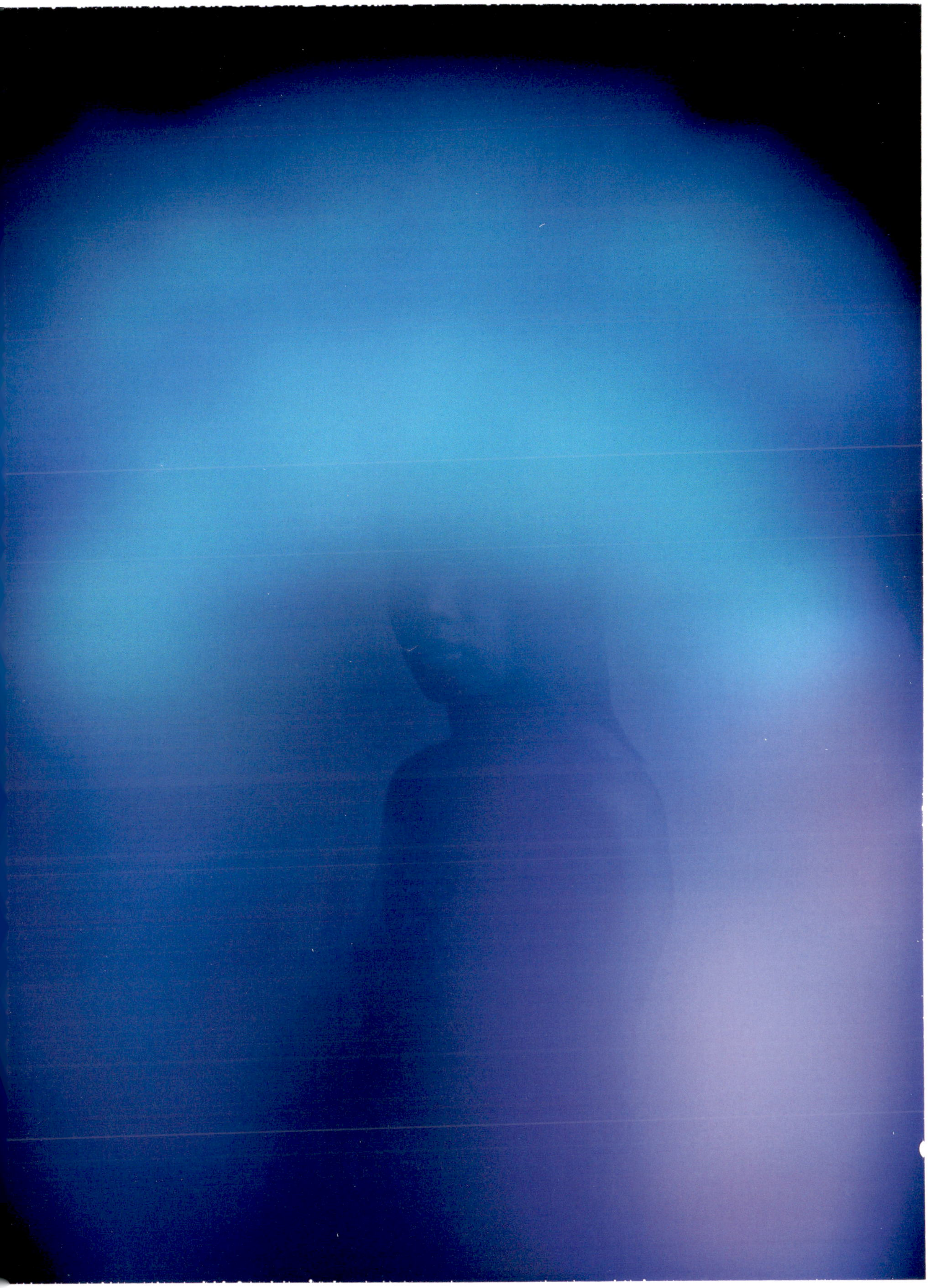

CENTER
ORANGE
Creative, Artistic

```
          *O*
      *O*     *O*
    *O*  .***.  *O*
   *O*  * @ @ *  *O*
   *O*  *  ,  *  *O*
   *O*  *( v )*  *O*
   *O*   *   *   *O*
  *O*  .**   **.  *O*
 *O*  *         *  *O*
*O*  * .*     *. *  *O*
*O*  * . *   * . *  *O*
*O*  * . *   * . *  *O*
*O*  * .  * *  . *  *O*
*O*  * . *   * . *  *O*
*O*  * .*     *. *  *O*
*O*  * .*     *. *  *O*
     *. *     * .*
     *..       ..*
```

RIGHT LEFT

ORANGE ORANGE

Creative, Artistic Creative, Artistic

**CENTER** (EXPERIENCE) Color above subjects head.
Indicates what the subject is experiencing. It is the color that would best describe them.
--Creative, artistic-- would best describe you. Orange represents energy with mental direction. You are alive, artistic, perceptive creative. Constructive self expression is important to you.

**RIGHT SIDE** (EXPRESSION) Color on subjects right.
Indicates the personality that the subject projects outward and how other people see them.
Creative endeavor, you are putting out and creating. Orange is a mixture of red --passion, force of will-- and yellow --cheerfulness--. The world should see you as up, happy, willing to work. You like to get out and have fun.

**LEFT SIDE** (FUTURE) Color on subjects left.
Indicates what the subject is creating for themself in the near future.
Activity generating energy is coming into your field. Orange is a mixture of active red and intellectual yellow, making a very creative future for you. Activity, wakefulness, and creativity unfolding. An opportunity to enjoy the sensual pleasures. Orange is known to give way to green, healing and growth, after the balancing period is over. Now is the time to go for it.

Martynka Wawrzyniak (Two), 2008.

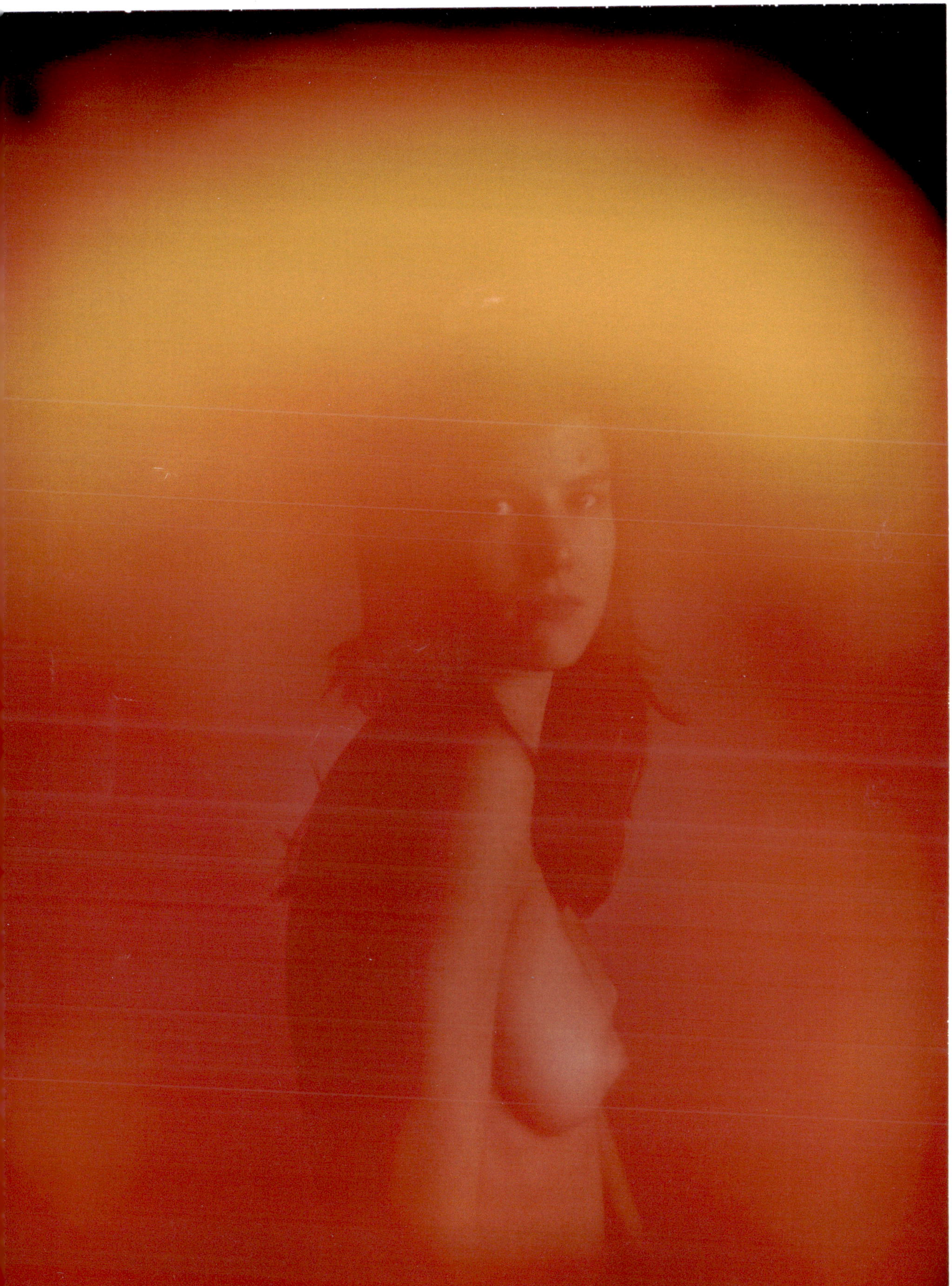

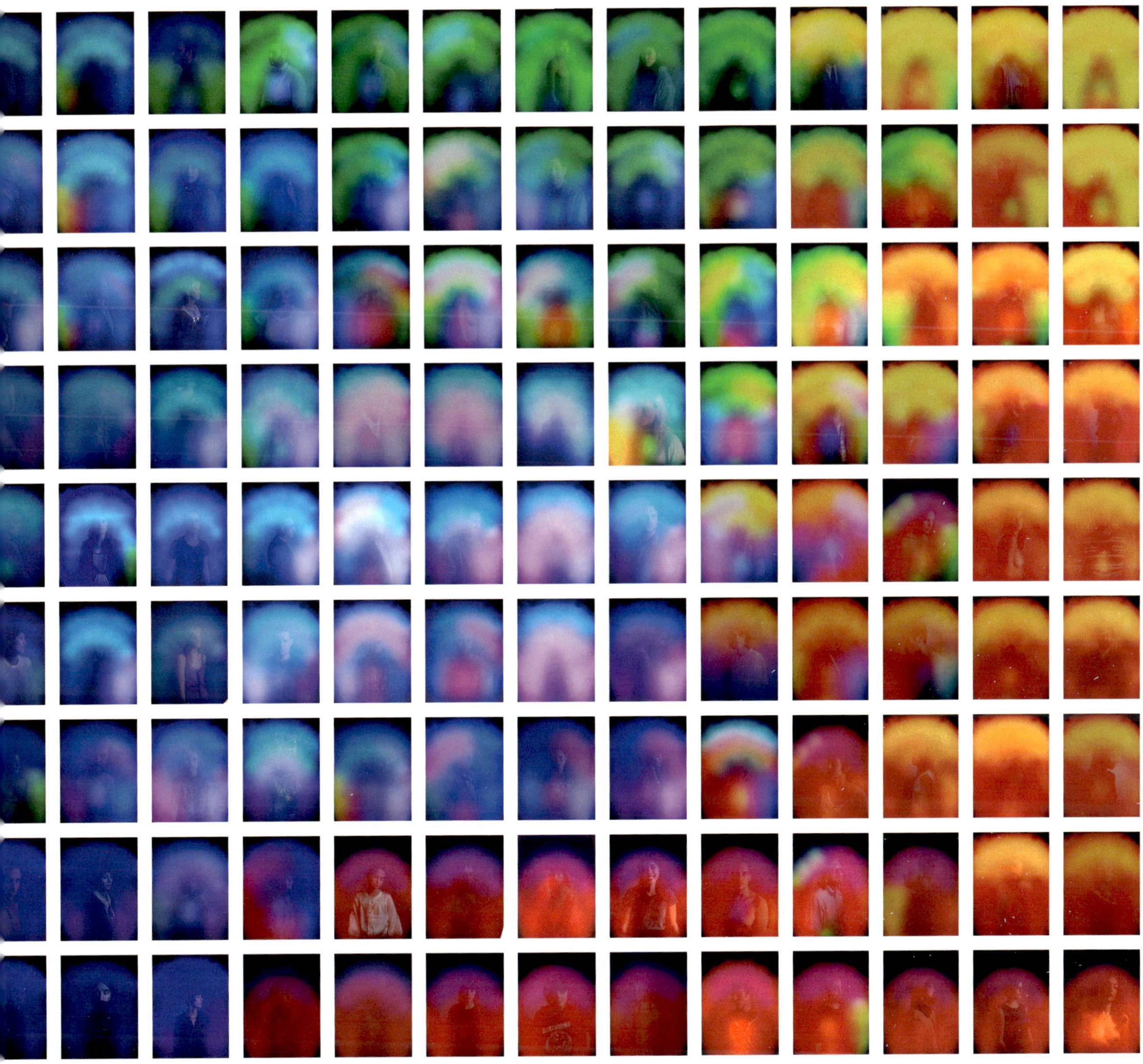

Grid, 2012.